'NEW BRITISH HISPANISMS'

Edited by Chris Perriam

T0386721

Contents

'Hispanism'. Introductory Remarks

In suggesting how the six contributors to this special issue meet with 'Hispanism' and produce further meanings for it, I need to comment on two very particular, and for some, no doubt, peculiar, limitations that I have placed on this collection of articles and to give a rationale for these. Firstly, all deal with Spain. For an exploration of new directions in the discipline this is risky, given that it was precisely British Hispanism's Eurocentrism that was one of its twin weaknesses ('anti-theoretical' canon-worship being the other) as it entered its first phase of transformational crisis in the 1970s, and given too the successive explosions of creativity and political commitment in imaginative writing and the diversity in thought among theorists in Spanish-speaking Latin America. But an awareness of just these contexts, just this exclusionary risk, refines any theorizing of 'Spain' and the study of Spanish culture: a set of cultural practices embedded in and mediated by a language—Castilian Spanish—that is the site of such diversity cannot but implicate all but the most obtuse of readers, viewers, listeners, consumers in an understanding of 'Spain' in terms of alterity, correlation, multiplicity. Thus all the contributors look both at and away from what is conventionally and canonically constructed as the subject matter of Hispanism or even its cautiously more open younger sibling Hispanic Studies.

Paul Julian Smith, in discussing current Anglo-American and Spanish Hispanisms, sees incompatibilities of theoretical emphasis and differences in scholarly agendas and academic tastes, and argues for a future common ground through engagement with the heterogeneous field of Spanish culture in a Bourdieu-based cultural studies approach. Smith's theoretically radical, heretical, rewriting of the field of Hispanism has made him one of Britain's most exciting and prolific professors in the institutionally marked out area of Modern Languages at its interface with theory and Film Studies. Similarly placed, with a professorship which is a tribute to and platform for her theoretical-historical and increasingly interdisciplinary pioneering work, Jo Labanyi turns to the Italian left to examine possibilities for the application of Gramsci's cultural theories to the study of Spain. She argues here that the variety and vitality of Spain's popular cultural traditions have, in the modern and postmodern eras, combined with the diverse forms of mass culture to produce a particularly interesting case of cultural hybridity and nation-formation.

The four other contributors are Hispanists who are younger in terms of career progression and present here what is, if by no means a complete sample of the range of radical practices in Hispanism in Britain, at least a set of exemplary excursions out across the familiar into the new. Jonathan Thacker re-assesses Spanish seventeenth-century drama—once, as part of 'Golden Age' studies, a favoured subject area of establishment Hispanism in Britain and Ireland, now scandalously unexploited—by interrogating critical positions both of Golden Age studies' traditional heyday here and their renaissance in the USA, and moving towards a new position from which to privilege performative contexts, returning to the drama as a popular art-form. Richard Cleminson, who like Labanyi has as one of his set of skills that of the radical historian, highlights a number of sites for future investigation around the question of homosexuality in Spain. The larger question now seems long consecrated, largely due to the Almodóvar and latterly the Lorca phenomena, in the work of Smith and others; where Cleminson moves urgently in new directions is in his insistence on a sociologically-informed genealogy attentive to cultural milieu and moment, and in his desire to look back beyond the glittering post-Franco years and ask whether it is possible 'to talk of "homosexuality" to refer to lifestyles, acts and identities forged over a period which spans perhaps more than one hundred years as though they were linked', in other words to remind other scholars in the field of the many strata they may unconsciously be walking over. David Vilaseca takes up a positive, sceptical, and dialectical position on cultural specificity in relation to an analysis of identity, sexuality and culture, focusing on the representation of homosexuality in Juan Goytisolo—now another of Hispanism's consecrated sites—and on his texts as revealing (or, rather, having revealed to them) what Žižek, after Lacan, calls an 'inverted message from the (big) Other'. Using the Hollywood disaster movie to explicate this position, Vilaseca deftly shows how high theoretical, and especially psychoanalytic, analyses can rescue Hispanism both from naïve calls to politicization (in certain empty gestures towards attentiveness to cultural specificity) and from its long fascination with just the text and author (a fascination which Vilaseca, like Smith elsewhere, allows himself provisionally to fall for precisely in order to know it).

Working from feminist ground and looking out toward both the popular fantastic and postmodern parodic, Vanessa Knights discusses how gender and cultural studies can be used productively to examine the formation of identities—both collective and individual—through discursive practices in fantasy and science fiction by Spanish women.

Like Smith (and Vilaseca) she insists on the potential in the production and critical consumption of narrative fiction for radical re-situations of the subject and new understandings of cultural specificity. She alerts us to the deconstructive dynamic set up between language and gender relations in the context of semi-popular literary writing and tacitly, and importantly, urges a greater sense of adventure on feminist readings of Spanish texts (for, as Labanyi argues, hispanists have concentrated for long enough on Spain's high culture, leaving aside the transactions between the different cultural forms).

It will have become clear from the résumé and the names above that a second deliberate limitation on the contributions is that all are written from within the institutional context of British (indeed, English) Hispanism. This is in order to continue to problematize that context, one whose political fortunes and critical affiliations are (in their small way) a theoretical treasure trove and one which, for the dissident practitioners within it, contains a cautionary history of exclusions, power games and *intereses creados* (vested interests) as well as acts of generosity, openness and commitment.

As late as the beginning of the current decade, Malcolm Read, in a set of essays aiming to move across the field of Hispanism towards 'a postmodernist Marxist theory of [the] genesis and formation of [the human subject] within a socio-economic environment', observed ruefully that '[British] Hispanism has never itself paused to consider its own institutional role or the ideological nature of its critical practice'.[1] This was despite the (probable) existence, earlier this century as also now, of what Smith suggests is a certain relative openness in Spanish Studies to experimentation ('lacking the high culture burden of French' as Smith puts it); despite the (evident) existence of scholars of enthusiasm and acuity whose writing was as often as not concerned to question received ideas and make a break with the facts-dates-and-editions tendency within of the highly institutionalized and patriarchal Hispanisms of other European countries; and despite at least one British voice, that of Barry Jordan, already raised in book-length dismay at the narrowness and political one-sidedness of the subject, at least in its pedagogical manifestations.[2]

The Association of Hispanists of Great Britain and Ireland's annual conference section on Literary Theory (which Jordan reminds us began in March 1982: *BHCLT,* 4) has petered out (that Literary label could neither appease the conservatives nor inspire the progressives); and it is still not uncommon to see in institutions of some prestige evidence of the fetishization in the teaching of undergraduates of 'private feelings, moral values, human experience, great literature, the individual and universal man' (Jordan, *BHCLT*, 85). Nonetheless, Smith was right to draw to the attention of his original US audience to 'a sea change in much UK Hispanism', one which this issue hopes to highlight through speculation and demonstration. The many exciting and significant projects to take Hispanism forward suggested by Labanyi through (neo-)Gramscian analyses of cultural transaction, intellectuals and their institutions and favoured genres, values and meanings for the 'national'; the interrogations of 'high', sociological, feminist, new historicist, and genre theories; *Paragraph*'s own interest itself in this field: all suggest a moment of transformation.

The change has come bewilderingly late, but it is now no longer true in most university departments in Great Britain and Ireland that Hispanism presents the 'narrow, highly selective and linguistically defective introduction to the culture(s) it studies' which Jordan saw at the end of the 1980s, an introduction 'relying almost exclusively on a literary access route' (*BHCLT*, 1). Although a literary canon (now not the 17th-century-oriented canon of the '50s to the '70s) and sometimes empirical philology too still provide the most usual structure, cinema is a common (and sometimes somewhat hastily erected) alternative walkway into acquired cultural awareness, and many of the 'new' universities (whose affiliation tends to be to the Association for Contemporary Iberian Studies, which is less concerned with literature) are able to bring to the discipline the multi-disciplinary advantages of Area or European Studies and of Media Studies. Another route into a fuller sense in both teachers and students of the cultures of Spain is opened up by staying with the textual but strategically marginalizing or through strong reading turning inside out the staid old—or new—emphatically literary (this has the not inconsiderable side benefit too, in a context where our undergraduate students are learning the language, of exposing them to words and inflections they might in fact encounter and want to use in their social transactions). In addition to the growing corpus of Spanish Film Studies (another story) and the strategies proposed or exemplified in the contributions which follow, it is worth recording that significant work has been and is being done in popular women's fiction of the 1940s and 50s (albeit sometimes undertaken only because of such fiction being signalled intertextually in more literary texts), in the alleyways that join detective fiction to postmodern narrative practice, and in a belated response to the intense interest within Spain itself in columnists and essayists in the (albeit high brow, small circulation) press.

At a significant number of places at what once were its boundaries, then, British Hispanism has reached beyond its literary critical heritage and beyond what Read less than a decade ago was describing as 'the point at which [it] would fall silent [. . .] when [it] threaten[ed] to open out upon social process' (*LTS*, 153). On the other hand, there is as yet a strictly limited number of individual non-Latin Americanist scholars who depart from the conventional analysis of text and image to engage in theoretical discourse around issues raised by either 'the subject' or 'the social'; and fewer still who in relation to their research sustain the questions: why? for whom? to what social and intellectual purpose? Our project in this issue is to pick up and amplify these too faint echoes and to continue to redesign, or—who knows?—abandon the chamber of our discipline.

CHRIS PERRIAM
University of Newcastle

NOTES

1. Malcolm Read, *Language, Text, Subject: A Critique of Hispanism*, (West Lafayette, Ind., Purdue University Press, 1992), pp. ix and 9. Henceforth referred to as *LTS*.
2. Barry Jordan, *British Hispanism and the Challenge of Literary Theory* (Warminster, Aris and Phillips, 1990). Henceforth referred to as *BHCLT*.

Towards a Cultural Studies of the Spanish State[1]

There is currently something of a boom in Hispanic studies in the UK. With continuing growth in undergraduate numbers and the opening of new departments, Spanish is rivalling German as second studied foreign language after French. The reasons for this increase are various: the realization that Spanish, like Portuguese or English, is at once a European Union language and a world language; the cumulative effect of thirty years of mass tourism and, more recently, mass migration by British citizens to Southern Spain; the perception that Spanish is pleasurable, reinforced by rare, but significant, mass cultural exports such as Almodóvar, Antonio Banderas, and Joaquín Cortés.

Beyond this boom in Hispanic studies, however, there has been a sea change in much UK Hispanism. A glance at the recent conference programmes of the Association of Hispanists of Great Britain and Ireland sees sessions on gender, race, popular culture, and technology which are the common coinage of the MLA; the newly split *Bulletin of Hispanic Studies* finds itself more responsive to areas such as queer theory. Many British Hispanists, once pragmatic and suspicious of abstraction, have fallen for theory in a big way. Where even ten years ago it was rare to meet a Professor of Spanish in a British university who was not a Medievalist, now it is rare to meet one who is. Recent elections to Chairs include specialists in film studies, feminism, poststructuralism, and cultural and gay studies. And unlike Pierre Bourdieu's 'consecrated heretics' in the France of the 1960s (figures such as Barthes or Derrida whose intellectual fame was matched only by their institutional marginality)[2] these new figures in British Hispanism combine intellectual and institutional prestige.

Moreover this institutionalization of once radical or anti-authoritarian positions looks likely to reproduce itself: changes in government funding mean that postgraduate students, whose apprenticeship was until recently controlled by their relationship with a single supervisor, now initiate their career with an MA (or in Cambridge an MPhil) whose compulsory 'core courses' are generally theoretical in nature; and the repeated Research Assessment Exercises initiated by the British government and directly linked to university funding have had the unintended effect of consolidating the power of those who are most active in research, who tend to be less traditional in their inclinations. While Bourdieu, again, stresses in *Homo Academicus* (79) the differences between intellectual and financial capital (for example, the former, unlike the latter, cannot easily be inherited by successors), the structural link between research and funding in British universities has to some extent rendered the two capitals equivalent. To take a hypothetical example, a monograph by a young scholar on Galdós and Žižek, which might once have been scorned by older colleagues as preposterous, could now save the financial life of a struggling Spanish department.

To return to the intellectual sphere, one advantage of British Hispanism is that it seems to lack the tension sometimes felt in the US between Peninsularists and Latin Americanists; indeed many of the consecrated heretics to whom I refer above (such as myself) teach and publish in both fields. And lacking the high culture burden of French, traditionally the lingua franca of the elite, Spanish, relatively neglected still, is free to pursue a more experimental agenda. The differing reception of French and of Spanish cinema in the UK in the last decade reveals the benefits of freedom from the prestigious but elitist burden of 'heritage'. However if the concerns of current British Hispanism, more politically engaged, would seem to be opposed to those of previous more moralizing times, then I would suggest that both new and old regimes find a certain common ground in ethics: while earlier critics saw poetic justice as the driving force of the comedia,[3] current scholars addressing gender, race, homosexuality, or popular culture are motivated by a sense of natural justice towards the dispossessed. If we would no longer wish away Calderón's wife murders claiming that the husbands contrive their own punishment by killing the thing they love, then we may still see the operation of poetic and natural justice in, say, Rosario Castellanos's dramatic narratives of subaltern and familial revolt.

It is clear that there is something of a divide between the concerns of many current British and Spanish Hispanists. This is somewhat ironic, given that some of the approaches only recently adopted in the UK had been pioneered in Spain (but outside Spanish universities) as far back as the 1970s. For example, current Anglo Spanish film studies has more in common with the film criticism of a non-academic journal such as *Contracampo* during the Transition than with the formalist film theory practised by some Spanish academics of the 1990s.[4] Or again, Spanish and Catalan lesbian and gay activist texts of the 1970s were more intellectually sophisticated than the queer theory which is only just emerging within a Spanish university context and is heavily indebted to US precedents.[5] There is no doubt, then, that the emigration of talented

Spanish scholars to the US (and to a lesser extent the UK) has been a grave loss to Spanish universities; indeed the intellectual differences between Spanish and Anglo-American Hispanists have sometimes re-curred between Spaniards who have remained at home and those working abroad.[6] It may be that the most fruitful collaborations be-tween Anglo-American Hispanists and scholars in Spain will take place not in departments of '*filología*' or '*literatura española*', but in depart-ments of communication, media studies, visual arts or, indeed, with independent intellectuals.

Of course many in Spain view much critical theory as a faded fashion of the 1970s, which, like the radical politics of the same period, was swiftly superseded.[7] This generational model is, however, descriptive rather than analytical, reducing the intellectual to the personal. And other responses by some Spanish Hispanists to the challenges of Anglo-American Hispanism are equally problematic. For example the sugges-tion that language occupies the central position of debate in Spain corresponding to the importance of gender in the US simply masks the fact that women's studies has not achieved the same status in Spain as it has abroad. Or again the proposal that there is a Spanish theoretical 'dif-ference' which cannot be reduced to foreign models is a smokescreen under cover of which certain foreign theorists (such as Todorov, Genette, and Greimas) can be privileged over others. Finally, the cen-trality of the study of Spanish literature to Spanish national identity has been invoked as an explanation for the relative lack of heretical readings of figures such as Cervantes in Spain itself. Indeed it would seem unde-niable that more is at stake for Spaniards working on and in their own culture than for those of us writing and working abroad. But this is not true in the comparable case of English studies in the UK, where the aca-demic study of homosexuality (one of the most controversial of areas) grew out of one of the most canonic and nationally invested of fields: Shakespeare studies.

But there is a theoretical basis to such questions of academic taste, one revealed by the pervasive use in Spain of 'scientific' as a positive term when applied to literary or cultural studies. While Spaniards re-main unwilling to abandon positivist authority (and the scientist theo-ries of structuralism and formalism), Anglo-Americans tend in their work to offer critiques of an objectivity held to be spurious and to adopt subjective positions which would, in Spain, undermine their au-thority. The clearest example is the apparent impossibility of calling oneself an academic feminist in Spain. Now it could well be argued, fol-lowing Bourdieu again, than to disavow one's academic authority, whether through the ironies of deconstruction and psychoanalysis or a more or less explicit identification with the socially subaltern positions of women or gay men, is merely to display mastery of the latest academic moves and discourses, simply to reinstate more securely one's own authority as a licensed heretic. It remains the case, however, that there is a social and political investment in much Anglo-American Hispanism which is incompatible with the intellectual and institutional traditions of much Spanish Hispanism. Hence while Anglo-Americans accuse Spaniards of immobilism, Spaniards accuse Anglo-Americans of faddism, of falling for any and every critical fashion.

From a Peninsular perspective, cultural studies must seem merely the latest of these successive fads, overdue for its fifteen minutes of academic fame. What I will be arguing, however, and more positively than in the first half of this paper, is that cultural studies (and more particularly the work of sociologist Pierre Bourdieu) offers a future common ground or lingua franca for Hispanists in Spain and abroad, most particularly in its attempt to integrate the historical and the theoretical. What is cultural studies? Let us begin with three premises, framed perversely perhaps as double negatives: first, cultural studies does not neglect the author or producer, although it does place him or her within the field of other texts, producers, and institutions; second, cultural studies does not neglect fantasy and desire, although it does suggest that subjective dispositions are inseparable from objective positions; third, cultural studies does not neglect elite or high culture, although it does explode the object of study to include any practice and representation of social life. These three premises correspond to three modes of cultural studies, focussing in turn on production, representation, and texts. Fortunately work has already been carried out in each of these modes of cultural studies in relation to the extraordinarily rich and varied field of Spanish culture after Franco. Thus Eduardo Subirats's intellectual and cultural histories of the period reveal how producers and institutions operate within a single field that is at once political and aesthetic.[8] Teresa Vilarós's articles and forthcoming monograph on the Transition reveal how motifs such as the feather or addiction are played out in representations motivated by both psychic fantasies and social structures.[9] Finally, I myself have continued to make close readings of elite literature, cinema, and visual art while also attempting to address the multiple and ephemeral media in which Spaniards have presented and represented such issues as the AIDS crisis.[10]

Ultimately such work, now being undertaken by a number of scholars, must address that most fragile and fascinating of phenomena: the texture of everyday life. But I would like to insist for a moment on the methodological difficulty of a contemporary Spanish cultural studies, a difficulty which is heightened by the lack of a Spanish tradition of cultural theory comparable to that produced in Germany or Italy. How do we focus on what has been called 'the spectacle of democracy'?[11] We need to avoid the twin perils suggested here by the double genitive. If, on the one hand, democracy is read as spectacle, then the social may be reduced to representation and its material effects neglected. If, on the other, the spectacle of the mass media is read as a mere tool of democracy, then the social may be divorced from representation and the productive force of the media neglected. What is vital, therefore, is that, caught between these two non-dialectical models of the relationship between culture and society, we do not simply map postmodern theory (with its now familiar themes of performance, particularity, and play) on to a Spanish cultural scene already thought quintessentially to embody those same themes. I would suggest, then, that one critical space or position which would provide some purchase on this most heterogeneous of objects is that offered by Bourdieu's analysis of the cultural field.

Bourdieu has not to my knowledge received a great deal of attention from Hispanists. And clearly his work has disadvantages for those of us trained in what we have received as 'French theory'.[12] First, as an empirically trained (but philosophically informed) sociologist, he is dismissive of what he brands the 'speculative' theory of the licensed heretics: from Barthes, Derrida, and Foucault to Frantz Fanon. Second, he is generally indifferent to the issues of gender, nationality, and homosexuality central to Anglo-American literary and cultural studies. Third, he is anaesthetic in style and dry to read, pointedly disdaining the 'brilliance' of an academic performance which he claims is merely a device internal to the workings of the academy. In spite of his conceptual complexity, then, Bourdieu refuses to seduce his intellectual disciples in the style of previous Parisian masters and mistresses.

What I would argue, however, is that Bourdieu offers a common ground for Anglo American and Spanish Hispanists. At a theoretical level, this is because his work is at once empirical and philosophical, historical and theoretical, particular and abstracted. Based on the most rigorous statistical analyses, Bourdieu's massive accounts of the academy, of the judgement of taste, and the rules of art are objective enough to satisfy the strongest Spanish proponent of 'scientific' positivism. But informed by a philosophical self-consciousness which submits his own position within the intellectual field to equally rigorous analysis (plotting his own position on the graphs of *Homo Academicus*), Bourdieu's works also conform to the poststructuralist and Anglo-American requirement for a reflexive awareness of the subject's implication in the object of study. Poised, like Marxism, between empiricism and idealism, but avoiding exhausted Marxist debates on ideology, base and superstructure, or hegemony, Bourdieu not only suggests a new dynamic model of the relation between the social and the cultural (with the 'field' as the space of interaction of texts, producers, and institutions); he also offers an exit for the dead end of much US cultural studies with its endless and often fruitless search for subversion.

It seems only fair to give a few pointers as to how Bourdieu's great 'architecture' of work might be of use to contemporary Spanish studies. One area would be an analysis of the role and position of Spanish intellectuals in the current cultural field.[13] Such a study would analyse the producers of *ensayo*, both academic and journalistic, in relation to the field of texts and institutions in which they operate; it would investigate how the objective conditions of intellectuals mesh with the subjective dispositions (fantasies and desires) of their colleagues and their audiences; and it would explode the distinction between the elite literary texts which are assumed to be of lasting value and the journalistic ephemera which produces and is produced by the practice of everyday life. The point of positing an 'intellectual field' in Madrid or Barcelona, then, (as in Bourdieu's Paris) is to suggest, against both Marxist totalization and postmodern 'play', the particularity of the general (with intellectuals bringing into focus the specific discursive configurations of the Transition) and the generality of the particular (with those broader implications uniquely expressed in intellectuals' versions of the contemporary problematic). It would not be to argue that figures such as Fernando Savater or Francisco Umbral, say, were inherently subversive in their heretical divergence from the discursive status quo or habitus; but nor would it be to propose that their texts are reducible to the institutional positions their producers inhabit. Rather it would be to analyse the overdeterminations through which producers, texts, and institutions effect and affect the multiple distinctions of which social and cultural life are composed.

A Bourdieu-based cultural studies of the Spanish state would thus be different from an approach based on the social sciences: firstly, in its promotion of a necessary eclecticism as the only means adequate to the extreme heterogeneity of its object of study; secondly, in it problematization of the relation between the subject and that object, the observer and the observed. The objectified ethnological approach (much criticized by Bourdieu) would thus be subjectivized by that close attention to fantasy and to representation which has been the particular strength of literary studies. If I venture to use the term 'structure of feeling' here it is not because I believe (like Raymond Williams) that cultural studies must be informed by a specific political programme or because I wish to return to a reified notion of popular or class-based 'experience'; but rather because in its tense and tender oxymoron the phrase hints at a fusion of the subjective and objective in which culture and society are practically indistinct and theoretically indistinguishable.

In the introduction to their invaluable *Spanish Cultural Studies* (whose contributors consist mainly of British Hispanists and Spanish media scholars) Jo Labanyi and Helen Graham argue that the particularly brilliant character of twentieth-century Spanish culture derives ultimately from what has often been seen as its greatest disadvantage: Spain's tardy, uneven, and accelerated modernization.[14] And it is no accident that the recent cultural exports I mentioned at the start of this paper (Almodóvar, Banderas, and Cortés) each hold in tense and tender combination, once more, aspects of modernity and tradition, mass and folk culture, the international and the local. If, then, UK Hispanism is to benefit from its current boom and if the differences between Peninsular and Anglo-Americanism Hispanisms are to be bridged, we will have to adopt or adapt some of the intellectual flexibility, even opportunism, that is characteristic of the many hued movement known as cultural studies and the manifold conceptual architecture of Bourdieu. Only then will we as scholars and teachers be worthy of the spectacular and contradictory brilliance of Spanish culture at the end of the twentieth century.

PAUL JULIAN SMITH
University of Cambridge

NOTES

1. This article was first read as a paper at the conference on 'Spanish Studies Today' held to inaugurate the King Juan Carlos I Center, New York University, New York City, in 1997.
2. Pierre Bourdieu, *Homo Academicus* (Cambridge, Polity, 1988), p. 105.
3. I refer to Alexander A. Parker, *The Approach to Spanish Drama of the Golden Age* (London, Diamante, 1957); for a critique of this once influential position see my *Writing in the Margin: Spanish Literature of the Golden Age* (Oxford, Oxford University Press, 1988), p. 129.

4. The heyday of *Contracampo* was the politicized 1970s; for contemporary formalist film studies see Santos Zunzunegui, *Paisajes de la forma: ejercicios de análisis de la imagen* (Madrid, Cátedra, 1994).

5. For a survey of the theoretical sources of Spanish queer activism in the 1970s see Lubara Guílver and Roger de Gaimon's preface to the translation of Jean Nicolas, *La cuestión homosexual* (Barcelona, Fontamara, 1982 [first published 1978]), pp. 9–16; for a recent collection representative of queer Spanish scholars working in a number of disciplines see *Conciencia de un singular deseo: Estudios lesbianos y gays en el estado español*, edited by Xosé M. Buxán Bran (Barcelona, Laertes, 1997).

6. *Spain Today: Essays on Literature, Culture, Society*, edited by José Colmeiro, Christina Dupláa, Patricia Greene and Juana Sabadell (Hanover, Dartmouth College, 1995) is the proceedings of a conference at which these differences were manifest.

7. See *Critical Practices in Post-Franco Spain*, edited by Silvia L. López, Jenaro Talens and Darío Villanueva (Minneapolis, University of Minnesota Press, 1994), p. xi.

8. See Eduardo Subirats, *Después de la lluvia: sobre la ambigua modernidad española* (Madrid, Temas de Hoy, 1993); and 'Postmoderna modernidad: la España de los felices ochenta', *Quimera* 145 (March 1996), pp. 11–18.

9. See Teresa Vilarós, 'Los monos del desencanto español', *MLN* 109 (1994), 217–35.

10. See my *Vision Machines: Cinema, Literature, and Sexuality in Spain and Cuba, 1983–93* (London, Verso, 1996).

11. Richard Maxwell, *The Spectacle of Democracy: Spanish Television, Nationalism and Political Transition* (Minneapolis, University of Minnesota Press, 1995); see also *Refiguring Spain: Cinema/Media/Representation*, edited by Marsha Kinder (Durham, N.C. and London, Duke University Press, 1997).

12. The general sketch of Bourdieu that follows derives from *Homo Academicus* and the following texts: *The Logic of Practice* (Cambridge, Polity, 1992); *In Other Words: Essays Towards a Reflexive Sociology* (Cambridge, Polity, 1994); *Distinction: A Social Critique of the Judgment of Taste* (London, Routledge, 1996); and, with Jean-Claude Passeron, *The Inheritors: French Students and Their Relation to Culture* (Chicago, University of Chicago Press, 1979).

13. I have recently published three articles rereading Spanish intellectuals in the light of Bourdieu: 'Back to front: Alberto Cardín's queer habitus', *Bulletin of Hispanic Studies* [Liverpool], 74 (1997), 473–81; 'Social space and symbolic power: Fernando Savater's intellectual field', *Modern Language Review* 93 (1998), 94–104; and 'Modern times: Francisco Umbral's chronicle of distinction', *Modern Language Notes* 113 (1998), 324–38.

14. Helen Graham and Jo Labanyi's *Spanish Cultural Studies: An Introduction* (Oxford: Oxford University Press, 1995), p. 17. Graham and Labanyi argue for a renewed attention to modernity in the face of the Spanish promotion of particularity and play as typically postmodern virtues.

Rethinking Golden-Age Drama: The *Comedia* and its Contexts

In the late sixteenth and early seventeenth centuries a hybrid form of theatre developed in Spain (principally thanks to the prolific and inventive poet-playwright Lope de Vega) and became known as the *comedia*. The form flourished throughout the country's golden century; and if we are to believe the editors of a recent *festschrift*, published in the United States, the study of the *comedia* 'enjoy[s] today what might be considered a Golden Age.'[1] In North America, as in the United Kingdom and Ireland, Hispanic Studies generally is a popular and growing academic discipline. Yet in the English-speaking countries on this side of the Atlantic the boom has not included medieval or Golden-Age studies but has been confined largely to Latin American and modern peninsular literature, film studies and cultural studies. The irony of this situation, whatever its causes, will not escape those British and Irish Hispanists who recall the figures who moulded and invigorated Hispanism here in the middle decades of this century through what has also been termed 'the "golden age" of *comedia* criticism'.[2] After figures such as Alec Parker, Edward Wilson, Terence May and Albert Sloman, we did not suddenly arrive in 'estos nuestros detestables siglos' (these our hateful times),[3] but as the next generation, heavily influenced by these figures, reaches retirement age, a crisis looms in *comedia* studies (and in Golden-Age studies as a whole).

In this paper I intend to investigate this crisis and offer some thoughts on the future direction of *comedia* studies. My point of view is that of an academic trained in the late 1980s and early 1990s in traditional British university departments which were only just awakening to developments in theory. It is necessary to stress that my perception of a decline in British and Irish *comedia* studies is somewhat impressionistic, based chiefly on informally marshalled evidence:[4] the paucity of research students in the discipline; the erosion of posts devoted specifically to Golden-Age studies (and hence the *comedia*); the small number of conferences organized on the *comedia* and the relatively small number of papers on the subject at the annual conference of the Association of Hispanists; and the tendency of undergraduates to choose to study other areas of Hispanic culture.

Several rethinks of Hispanism (whether general or specific to the Golden Age) were published in Britain at the end of the 1980s and beginning of the 1990s in response to the challenge of theory. They were written mainly by supporters of theory who felt that (Golden-Age) Hispanism was moribund partly as a result of its practitioners' resistance to developments in theory, the implications of which were at least being discussed within its sister disciplines. The link was sometimes made explicit. In 1988 Paul Julian Smith claimed that 'British Hispanism especially has tended towards a formalism and moralism which can seem oppressive'.[5] He wrote of a possible 'renaissance' in Golden-Age studies which he correctly predicted would occur in North America (*Writing*, 6). Two years later Barry Jordan remarked that 'despite some notable exceptions, British Hispanism, in its institutional fabric and day-to-day workings, remains largely untouched by the theoretical revolution'.[6] He tentatively suggested a shift 'towards some sort of Cultural Studies' (*British Hispanism*, 105) as a way of revitalizing Hispanic Studies.[7] Peter Evans, in a tactfully worded article, urged British *comedia* scholars to moderate the 'somewhat exaggerated caution' they feel towards theory, and to 're-store the dramatists of this period to [their] contexts (...)—especially the contexts of ideology as an unconscious process'.[8] And George Mariscal, one of the most judicious of the supporters of theory to write on the Spanish Golden Age, decried '[t]he refusal within English-speaking Spanish studies to see that early modern literature in Spain may have had a political function, that is, local rather than universal' ('An Introduction', 20).[9] Both Evans and Mariscal clearly looked forward to the New Historical approaches to the *comedia* which North-American criticism has begun to produce in the 1990s (see below).

Although these important historicizers and prophets of Hispanism are overtly concerned with making scholars question their practices, with opening up a world of possibilities, they usually at least implicitly suggest that through resisting modern theoretical approaches (Golden-Age) scholars are responsible in part for the neglect their subject has fallen into.[10] Yet the source of responsibility for failure may not be the maligned complacent liberal humanist scholar, who measures his texts against inherited notions of universal man and human nature. We need to be more precise about what is 'wrong' with *comedia* studies in Britain and Ireland.

Is the decline even connected to the approaches taken by British and Irish critics of the *comedia*? Whether the comparatively small numbers of students choosing courses at undergraduate level and enrolling for

research degrees in Golden-Age studies is cause or effect of the diminu-
tion of Golden-Age posts in our university Spanish departments is unclear. Have the *comedia* specialists in these countries really, like the
silk-worm, built the house in which they will die? Clearly this possibility needs to be addressed but the question is more complex. Other factors to be considered include (in no particular order of priority): the
decline in textual study at A-level and its equivalents in recent years, especially of works regarded as 'difficult', which can be seen as part of a
stress on other (more utilitarian) areas of language learning (notably
oral and listening skills); the modularization of courses in our universities which often allows students a greater choice in the structure of
their degree; a broadening of the curriculum which provides the student with a growing diversity of courses from which to choose; the
proliferation of combined studies degrees (including the rise in European Studies) which decrease or change specialization; cultural
changes, specifically the familiarity of students with visual aspects of
culture, rather than written culture, which goes hand in hand with a
decline in reading (especially of non-contemporary texts); equations of
the modern with the relevant and the ancient with the obscure;[11] a
stress on vocational relevance and transferable skills rather than on the
study of art for art's sake; and more specifically, the lack of a performance tradition for Golden-Age plays in this country (equivalent to,
say, that for French Classical drama), the erosion of the Spanish depart-
mental play in universities, and the paucity of adaptations for the screen
of these plays (in marked contrast to the treatment of Shakespeare, for
example).

Superficial conclusions deduced from the North-American 'success-
story' may also be misleading. Is it a coincidence that interest in *comedia*
studies in the US has grown at a time when North-American critics are
reading the *comedia* from a variety of theoretical perspectives?[12] Would a
similar boom in Golden-Age studies occur here if most or all specialists
brought modern theory to bear on their study of the *comedia*? To what
extent is the North-American boom in Hispanic Studies (after all,
partly the result of demographic phenomena) general, and to what extent particular to *comedia* studies? What is the influence of North-
American university curricula, and particularly the broad postgraduate
programmes of study? How crucial is the comparatively high number
of American students with Spanish as a native language? Is the *comedia*
more accessible in the US? The causal connection between approach
and appeal is by no means evident, as some North-American scholars
acknowledge, and the issue needs further study.[13]

Rethinking the approach we take as critics to a subject area is important for a number of reasons. Thus far I have concentrated primarily on the suggestion, implicit or explicit in some criticism of the discipline, that *comedia* studies in Great Britain and Ireland have suffered from an outmoded approach (inherited from the patriarchs of British Hispanism, whose studies were often rooted in the Golden Age), which has contributed to their decline. A decline is easier to measure in quantitative than qualitative terms, and the evidence I have provided for the existence of a decline in *comedia* studies in Britain and Ireland has concentrated on scarcity of this and reductions in that. The imperatives of the day are apt to make one conscious of figures. The consumer-friendly culture in which we live makes it wise to popularize in order to survive, to present an up-to-date face. Yet a rethink of *comedia* studies should not concentrate solely on ways of enticing students into the subject (with the future growth that this implies), and ways of competing for attention with film studies and Latin American studies.[14] As already stated, approaches to the *comedia* in the undergraduate classroom and in the journal may differ considerably for a number of reasons. Those critics who called for an increase in the application of theory to Golden-Age texts did so not only with the aim of changing how we teach the *comedia* to a new generation but out of the ideological conviction that there was much to be gained from the perspectives provided by the new approaches developing within literary studies and especially other disciplines such as anthropology, philosophy, psychology, political, gender and communication studies. They lamented a reluctance even to consider the new (even if consideration led to rejection),[15] and to see the need to defend traditional critical standpoints. The battle has something of the generational conflict of Golden-Age comedy about it.

Whilst I would not go so far as to claim that this article will provide a comic anagnorisis, it is nevertheless true that thinking about the future direction of British and Irish *comedia* studies is, in some ways, an easier task now than it was for critics ten or so years ago. This is because the 'renaissance' which Smith foresaw in North-American Golden-Age studies allows us to see the strengths and weaknesses of new theoretical approaches, as well as focusing more clearly on the values inherent in some traditional approaches. Some dust has settled. Broadly, modern approaches can be divided into two groups: theoretical criticism (e.g. feminist, Marxist, deconstructive), which involves reading the *comedia* from a particular stance or set of beliefs, and the New Historicism, a reaction to some post-structuralist approaches, which posits a specific view of history (influenced by Marxism) and its relationship to literature.

I intend briefly to evaluate both of these approaches as they have been applied to the *comedia* by North-American critics. I will base this evaluation on two recently published volumes of articles broadly representative of the two approaches. Barbara Simerka, the editor of the first, which is entitled *El arte nuevo de estudiar comedias*, divides the essays into three sections which characterize the approaches taken by the contributors: 'Poststructuralism and the *Comedia*', 'Cultural Studies and the *Comedia*' and 'Eclectic Approaches'. The aim of many of the contributors is, according to Simerka, to provide 'a defense of the usefulness of literary theory in general, and of their chosen approach in particular, for enriching the study of the *comedia*' (*El arte nuevo*, 7). The verb 'enrich' will not be read without irony by the sceptic who will understand the term as involving an unprincipled supplementing of value, rather than an (archaeological) discovery of something (of value) that was 'already there'.

Such scepticism would not be entirely misplaced. Simerka's volume illustrates clearly the problems as well as the benefits of taking theoretical approaches to the *comedia*. We shall deal with the problems first. When put into practice, the theoretical approaches in this collection, with their stress on subjectivity, their hostility to the notion of fixed meaning and authority in the text, their suspicion of the 'assumptions that we bring to our literary endeavors' (Simerka, 'Introduction', 10), their tendency to overinterpret, nevertheless often ultimately fail to escape the appeal to objectivity, to common-sense interpretations which theorists object to in traditional criticism (e.g. Parker's). The trace is, I suppose, inevitable. Despite the acknowledgement of the Derridean abyss in which, in Grace Burton's words, 'there can be no origin, no truth, no being that is itself not a product caught in an infinite regress from which there is no escape,'[16] these theorists are still often required, in order to say anything at all about their plays, to appeal to notions which universalize, which link them to their readers' and to other past and present critics' beliefs which give them a context in which to express themselves. Occasionally the novelty and originality of the article is in the explanation of the approach, rather than the conclusions arrived at about the play.[17]

A number of other problems emerge from these theoretical readings of the *comedia*. Theoretical approaches can leave the reader better informed about the relevant theory than the supposed object of study. The typical pattern of the criticism in Simerka's volume is a setting out of the theory (which can stretch to over half of the article) followed by an application of it to the play(s) in question. This means that as well as elucidating an aspect of the play, the critic applies an extra layer of difficulty or complexity to it. This problem will surely become less severe as individual theories become more widely known and require less introduction. For the time being it is a difficult task for the 'traditional' critic effectively to engage with and criticize theoretical approaches to the *comedia*, without expending much time and energy becoming acquainted with the theory in depth.[18] Often this process will seem superfluous where the critic cannot perceive the advantages of the new approach in terms of greater appreciation or understanding of a play.

Mariscal, amongst others, makes us aware that the application of theory to text can seem arbitrary ('History and the Subject', 21).[19] Many of the contributors to Simerka's volume, including Simerka herself, also warn of the dangers of misusing theory. The contributions are frequently couched in the rhetoric of caution and defensiveness, perhaps characteristic of the first stages of change, but which can betray a lingering consciousness of doubt.[20] Theoretical critics are aware no doubt that, if, in Smith's words, 'formalism and moralism can seem oppressive', then the theoretical revolution can seem liberating to the point of being carnivalesque. Criticism can become an intellectual game, in which the same text can be dressed up and undressed in a variety of colourful outfits. Interestingly the contributors do not often attempt to explain the rules to be applied to matching text with theory, in deciding which costume will suit, perhaps because that process itself has to call upon notions of common sense. The application of theory-based criticism to the world of the *comedia* requires further justification.

In addition to the problems already outlined, theoretical approaches to the *comedia* must confront the following questions: has the critic invented the outcome before doing the research?; has s/he forced a reluctant play to meet his/her own pre-existent expectations?; how does the critic cope with the anachronistic practice of applying modern theory to ancient texts?;[21] is the critic imposing unlikely aims on the dramatist in question (perhaps through excessive admiration)?; does the play's context undermine the theoretical conclusion?; has the play been read merely as a literary text or has its status as drama been taken into account?; do the modern demands of academic life to publish and progress pressurize the critic either into being sensationalist, or into applying a theory several times to different texts without discrimination?

Notwithstanding the above, the iconoclasm of theoretical criticism has done the *comedia* a service, however sceptical one remains about poststructuralist approaches to individual texts. Critics are less ready to accept overarching, monolithic theories, whether Parkerian or Maravallian,[22] and this seems healthy given the obvious diversity of the period and genre in question. Theoretical criticism has exploited the margins of the text to foreground issues in the *comedia* which have been neglected but which were and are important. The spotlight has shone in a sustained fashion for the first time on women,[23] on sexuality, on religious and ethnic minorities, on the political and social content of the drama, and sometimes on the potential within performance.[24] Ambiguities have been exploited, textual gaps filled, hidden messages decoded, possibilities explored. Perhaps the greatest benefit of theory, however, is that it facilitates 'metacriticism' (Friedman, 'Theater Semiotics', 69); it makes us interrogate the means which we are using to explicate the text, be aware that no approach is value-free. As we have mentioned, one of the great frustrations of the innovators, expressed as long ago as 1974 by Parr ('An Essay'),[25] has been a perceived refusal on the part of 'traditional critics' to question their approaches, to analyse the assumptions lying behind them, including the intentionality of the author, the twin *points de repère* of human nature and universal man, the inviolability of their (reading of the) text.

One of the reactions to poststructuralism and its perceived failings is the New Historicism which in the UK and USA appeared initially (and predictably) in English Studies (and especially Shakespeare Studies). New Historicism has come to *comedia* studies more swiftly than did poststructuralism (partly, perhaps, as a result of the existence of a newly theory-literate body of *comedia* specialists); hence, for example, the short gap between the publication of Simerka's volume (1996) and the 1997 collection of essays edited by Madrigal (see note 12). New Historicism attempts to return the text to its context. The context is distinguished from that of earlier Historicism, which would place the work within a totalizing system, a 'linear development of literary history', as Margaret Greer expresses it.[26] New Historicists mistrust monolithic interpretations of history, and view the *comedia* as part of the 'trivia' which are traditionally 'excluded or marginalized' from historical narrative.[27] The text then helps us to understand a historical moment in all its tension. The approach can even be taken to the *auto sacramental* (allegorical religious drama), as Greer shows when she commits the 'heresy' of 'doubting the absolute transcendence of this [. . .] drama' ('Constituting Community', 41).[28] The method of analysis allows the critic still to exploit the suggestions buried in the text, but encourages their association with the milieu that brought them forth, as influenced by and influential within their world. New Historicism is aware both of the fact that the context is essential to the text, and that as critics historicizing these texts we are never fully able to escape our own context. In Stephen Greenblatt's terms, borrowed by a hispanist, we study the *comedia* 'by analogue to ourselves'.[29]

If, at first sight, the return of the context to the *comedia* is welcome, and merely attaches the importance to socio-historical contextualization that many critics already knew to exist,[30] New Historical approaches are themselves open to criticism on a number of levels. Because of New Historicism's mistrust of the canon, and of the value judgement, dramatic texts tend to be viewed as documents (admittedly often privileged above other forms of writing) useful in building up a picture of a contestatory historical moment, rather than as aesthetic objects. The mode of criticism, certainly in Madrigal's volume, tends also to ignore the play as performance, and see it primarily as text. The return of the context together with the denuding of the art object have allowed New Historicists a useful space in which to operate. Non-canonical plays have been studied without the value judgements of old to haunt them (although we have still only scratched the surface of the Golden-Age drama and most critical interest continues, unfortunately, to be in the twenty or so canonical plays of the period); neglected issues and new possibilities have been discovered within play texts; and there has been a much-needed emphasis on the political and social aims of drama (which of course can be overplayed in the rush to look for modern relevance in a work, or a modern consciousness in a long-dead playwright).[31]

So how should we study and teach the *comedia*? Theoretical approaches have revealed some of the limitations of 'traditional' criticism; New Historicism provides the socio-historical context missing in some theoretical criticism, but treats the artistic work as just another document and, in focusing too narrowly, can miss the multiplicity of readings possible within a dramatic work. The reticence and reservations explicit and frequent in both collections of essays on the *comedia* reveal an awareness amongst practitioners that late twentieth-century approaches do not, indeed cannot, provide some elusive master key for the interpretation of Golden-Age drama. Neither, however, do the results of the approaches unveil a *vestuario* (discovery space) tableau of the *comedia* bled to death by an unscrupulous and untrustworthy surgeon. In an article of 1991, Parr identified three ways that critics had been wont to approach the *comedia*, through *erudición*, *crítica* or *teoría*, and called for 'una visión sincrética, de conjunto, que incorpore lo mejor de las tres sin privilegiar a ninguna' ('a syncretic vision which incorporates the best of the three without privileging any one in particular').[32] Parr's broadmindedness is exemplary and is echoed by critics such as Blue and Friedman, amongst others, who refuse to become slaves to an approach for its own sake. These critics are anxious to maintain a broad perspective, which, although inevitably itself inscribed within their discourse, remains open and capable of accepting insights from whatever source.

Comedia scholars do have a responsibility to the propagation of their subject, to seek growth in the popularity of their discipline, to encourage the reading and performance of Golden-Age plays, but they also have a moral responsibility to the subject. We must weigh up carefully the benefits and disadvantages of any new approach to our field. Let us take an example to illustrate the problem. An article or a class on, say, Tirso de Molina's *Don Gil de las calzas verdes* (*Don Gil of the Green Breeches*) in which the *comedia* scholar concentrates on the cross-dressed female protagonist to prioritize modern theoretical issues of gender and masquerade, in order to explore the possibility that the play brings into question early-modern constructs of masculinity and femininity, is calculated to appeal to one who lives in a world in which these questions are regularly debated, part of the cultural backdrop. Such an approach could be a resounding success which opens up an early seventeenth-century work to an otherwise recalcitrant readership or public. There is no doubt that many of the plays of the Spanish Golden Age can be profitably examined in terms of power relationships, of class, sex and race, but surely producing a generation of students who see Golden-Age drama primarily in these terms is problematic. An approach which acknowledges the continued relevance of the play (its way of challenging a modern readership or audience) and its potentially subversive role in its day, but which tries to contextualize it in its performative, generic, social, political and historical contexts does more justice to the play. I am aware that my use of the phrase 'does more justice to', opens me up to the charge that I am appealing to the faded deity of universal objective common sense, and so I shall explain myself, by persevering with the example of *Don Gil de las calzas verdes*.

The student who leaves the class and writes an essay on proto-feminism in Tirso's play (or the interested reader who follows the article's argument) can explain how Tirso (arguably) reveals the constructed nature of gender roles, and hence patriarchal structures, (perhaps) in Spain in the early seventeenth century. S/he can have read the play closely and critically. The fact that Tirso would not necessarily understand the terms of the class/paper is of course unimportant—he would not necessarily have understood the terms of Parker's famous 'approach' to Golden-Age drama either.[33] Tirso has supplied us with thought-provoking material which individuals can relate not only to modern debates on sexual equality and sexuality but also to their own behaviour. What is lacking in such an approach is any attempt to understand the work in anything more than a superficial context. By this I do not necessarily mean that the work must be understood in terms of authorial intention, or the play of imagery, but, through situating the work in its various contexts, a great deal more, perhaps equally relevant, can be learned. A more rounded understanding of the play can emerge. Let us look at the possibilities raised by the five (sometimes overlapping) contexts mentioned above (viz. performative, generic, social, political and historical). As Gordon Minter reminds us, the first production of *Don Gil* was a disaster: 'It was a flop. How could it have been otherwise, Tirso laments, when Valdés [the actor-manager] had cast his overweight middle-aged wife as the quicksilver young lover Don Gil.'[34] This perhaps unusual context of performance throws a feminist reading of *Don Gil* into a new light and increases our understanding of the play's possible reception. We realize that the very lack of femininity in the woman playing a man probably caused the play to fail—the primitive audience required the cross-dressed woman to reveal her feminine graces not her masculinity. This knowledge can deepen our reaction to the play—revealing the proto-feminist reading as superficial (not wrong, but lacking profundity). The audience would surely react in different ways to different actresses. What does this reveal about the priorities of the audience? Is it the majority male section of the audience which determines failure and therefore in this case prejudices the transmission of a potentially feminist message to the *cazuela* (the women's part of the Golden-Age playhouse's auditorium)? How relevant is the actress today? The question of genre is also a key one. The tradition of comedy as socially corrective is important—not only does it help us read the play as a critique of early-modern materialism (also its social context and perhaps the key to a New Historical reading of the play), but it helps us to uncover the generational conflict (i.e. youth versus old age, young values versus old) which is perhaps more prevalent in the play than the sexual conflict (man versus woman) which we recognize more readily today in our own social context. None of these readings precludes our modern reading—a modern director is perfectly entitled to prioritize the feminist possibilities within the play, to make a comment upon today's society, perhaps—but they deepen our understanding of the play and help us to make informed judgements about it. They should certainly not be ignored in a study of the play.

Contextualization of a work can provide the opening for a more imaginative, and a more subtle reading of it, which may not be more 'right', but which does the text more justice, by allowing interpretation on more than one level, a plurality of approach. For example, Blue suggests that comedies of the 1620s in Madrid reflect in their hostility to arranged marriages a post hoc rejection of the regime of Philip III (the context of *Don Gil*), and, in their self-expression, a welcoming of what seemed to be the meritocracy of Philip IV and Olivares (*Spanish Comedy*, 85–6). Here historical knowledge is useful to provide background for the text. According to Blue, the comedies of the 1620s, despite their apparent similarities 'were different from those done in the 1630s or 1640s' (vii). A lack of historical knowledge might contribute to a failure to appreciate the play.

Almost all new approaches to literature react to what has preceded them. Critics who see themselves as aloof from this process (of absorption and re-elaboration) lack Friedman's metacritical perspective. Individual critics' ideas of what (they think or have been taught that) the *comedia* is, and perhaps what drama, literature or culture are, will go a long way to explaining their approach to Golden-Age drama. Just as the dramatist and the work 'are both within their time and system, constituted by and constitutive of their social, economic, political, cultural milieu even as they engage in a discussion of issues that transcend their topical limitations' (Blue, 'Calderón's *Gustos*', 37), so critics, willy-nilly, engage with and are engaged in their time. It is in a series of contexts then that I outline some ideas on the future direction of *comedia* studies: some already admitted to above, others no doubt unconscious, others that will become clearer perhaps as the years pass, or that are clearer to others than to me. These are not part of a proposal to replace other approaches, but a statement of the need to take more account of certain aspects of the *comedia* whose importance has been underplayed.

I should admit immediately to four certain influences on the last section of this essay: first, a scepticism about the application of some modern theory to Golden-Age drama; second, an interest in the practice of translating Golden-Age plays into English; third, the release of Pilar Miró's cinematic version of Lope de Vega's *El perro del hortelano* (*The Dog in the Manger*) (1996); fourth, reading the writings on the theatre of Peter Brook. The first reminds me, by default, of the value of looking at the play firstly (although not solely) in its sixteenth- or seventeenth-century contexts (especially of performance); the second reveals the technical skills of the playwright as he goes about his art, and the variety within even a single play; the third and fourth emphasize the importance of its performance to the meaning of a play. The *comedia* has been and is being studied in these terms by some critics, but these chiefly performative contexts are currently overshadowed by thematico-structural, theoretical and New Historical traditions.

There is space here to be suggestive and sweeping rather than detailed and precise—further justification for what follows must be set aside for analyses of individual plays, or can be read in the scholarship of some of the critics I quote. By performative contexts I mean not so much those of say, history, genre and censorship (although these are all important), but of acting, staging, costume, verse, music and wit in the play's performance. And I would also stress the significance of the composition of the audience and its reaction to the drama. Investigating these contexts can sometimes help us to an enhanced understanding and interpretation of the *comedia*, re-establishing it as a lively popular art-form which is also formally and intellectually rigorous.

Parr's 1975 complaint that 'almost never is the fact mentioned, in literary criticism, that [Golden-Age plays] were indeed written to be performed before an audience' ('A Reply', 484)[35] echoes Peter Brook's earlier general gripe about 'the scholar who emerges from routine performances of the classics smiling because nothing has distracted him from trying over and confirming his pet theories to himself, whilst reciting his favourite lines under his breath'.[36] Performance can be an obstacle to neat interpretations. Brook's perspective is useful because he is a theatre director whose job involves distinguishing between a play script and the play in performance, and because he writes about the drama of Shakespeare with an understanding that we can readily apply to the drama of Shakespeare's Spanish contemporaries. Brook prioritizes performative contexts in a way that few *comedia* critics do. He can remind us that

the sort of play that Shakespeare offers us is never just a series of events: it is far easier to understand if we consider the plays as objects—as many-faceted complexes of form and meaning in which the line of narrative is only one amongst many aspects and cannot profitably be played or studied on its own (102)

Similarly, '[t]he mistake would be to take events or episodes from a play and question them in the light of some third outside standard of plausibility—like "reality" or "truth" ' (102). The play acts in the present of its being viewed, and it acts through its performative contexts—'[t]he meaning will be for the moment of performance' (106).

Brook sees the theatre as essentially interacting in a complex way with the society in which it is performed,[37] but denies that this must make it realistic. He takes his examples of how theatre can succeed from Shakespeare and the stage for which he wrote, which was unadulterated by the expectations we bring to the theatre today in a culture with a knowledge of cinema and television. Brook emphasizes the power of the word—its creativity in a theatrical context (42), and its potential for creating a picture which in our image-based culture, is always done for us, 'today writers seem unable to make ideas and images collide through words with Elizabethan force' (54). He adds: '[f]or centuries, unrealistic speech has been universally accepted, all sorts of audiences have swallowed the convention that words can do the strangest things' (58).[38] He also stresses the advantages of minimal stage decoration, 'useless information absorb[s] our attention *at the expense of something more important*' (84, emphasis in original). We should not need 'creaking machines' (90) to move us from place to place.

Of course these points can be applied to the performance of the *comedia* and its listening audience, especially given the performing conditions of the *corral* theatres. The analysis of Golden-Age play texts ought to take into account not just the ideas as expressed (or repressed) by the speaking characters, but the staging of individual plays, their use of polymetry, the actors and their craft, the relationship between audience and actors, the use of language to evoke mood and location, including the use of songs, and the use of wit to shed light on meaning, or as an end in itself.[39] As critics we often try to reach conclusions about the *comedia* by discussing the ideas it contains. A study of its performative contexts may help us reach conclusions and interpretations, but it may also make us see the *comedia* acting as theatre. In a more recent work, Brook tries to explain that this 'cannot be an intellectual, least of all a rational process. The theatre is in no way a discussion between cultivated people. The theatre, through the energy of sound, word, colour and movement, touches an emotional button that in turn sends tremors through the intellect'.[40]

This mystery of the link between audience and theatrical performance will perturb many a critic. The scientific connection between emotion and intellect is not observable, the effect of the play not measurable, but, for Brook, this is where the power of theatre lies. What is certain is that the play operates, takes effect through a combination of influences on the eye and the ear. We ignore at our peril the formal elements of the *comedia* which helped (and can still help) the dramatist, the *autor de comedias* (actor-manager) and the cast to bewitch the audience.

The treatise or the sermon (and to a lesser extent the *auto sacramental*) with their different rhetorical strategies were written and spoken to persuade the intellect. The *comedia*, we must constantly remind ourselves (especially when we see relatively few performances), is a play which makes us feel. A particular speech should not automatically be taken at face value, its content interpreted through the lens of some 'reality' or 'truth'. This content can be undermined or modified by its form, or the contexts of its delivery, for example whether it is delivered at a whisper or with an accompanying wink.

The most obvious (and most obviously neglected) performative context is the *comedia's* polymetry and its effects on pace, mood, style, or the ear of the audience.[41] The born actor, Pedro de Urdemalas, of Cervantes's play of the same name, explains to his *autor* that the actor, 'A los versos ha de dar/valor con su lengua experta' ('To the poetry must, with his expert tongue, lend power').[42] There is no doubt, as more than one commentator has pointed out, that the many exceptions to Lope's eight lines on versification in his *Arte nuevo de hacer comedias* (*New Art of Writing Plays*), do not disprove the rule that 'los versos' ('the poetical forms') are relevant to 'los sujetos que va tratando [el poeta]' ('the subjects with which [the dramatic poet] deals').[43] Critics rarely comment on the significance of verse forms; editors usually list them in an introductory sub-section and move on to the bibliography. Yet if we discover, say, in a comedy, that the young men and the young women tend to speak in one metre and the older characters tend to speak in another, does this not make it more likely, whatever their words, that the play depicts generations rather than sexes in conflict? An attempt at a feminist interpretation of such a comedy must surely take this into account. To give a more specific example, the King in Cervantes's *Pedro de Urdemalas* expresses his passionate love for the gipsy, Belica, in *redondillas* (the traditional octosyllabic four-line verse recommended by Lope for love scenes). When he comes to persuade the queen that her jealousy is misplaced, he comically undermines the words of his denial by continuing in the same poetic form. The poetry has a direct effect on characterization in this case.[44] More significantly still, what are the implications of the *comedia* being poetic drama rather than 'naturalistic' drama? Does the fact that characters speak poetry remove them from a direct relationship with reality, or does it enhance or distil reality?

Before concluding, let us look briefly at some examples of other performative contexts whose study can aid interpretation of the *comedia*. As Louise K. Stein has recently noted, music in the *comedia* is not merely decorative, a dramatic filler, 'most of the songs in Lope's plays serve more than one function. The same song might aid in the formal delineation of a scene, serve verisimilitude, and indirectly introduce an important message or theme in relation to the plot'.[45]

Decisions about the staging of a *comedia* will also be fundamentally important for its meaning. Any interpretation or production of a play should take into account the conditions of its original staging, not to reproduce them necessarily, but because certain scenes are more comprehensible when visualized on the curtainless, apron stage of the *corral* theatre. The seemingly endless seconds that Teodoro leaves Diana fallen on the steps as she leaves the gondola in Miró's attentive film version of *El perro del hortelano* are as eloquent as a speech about their feelings for each other, their hesitations, their relative situations. A glimpse of a bloodied Mencía (the murdered wife of *El médico de su honra*, [*The Physician of his Honour*]) in a *vestuario* tableau, or even a bloodied sheet can be more horrifying than the full melodrama of the dead wife dragged on stage on her blood-soaked bed by her husband, Gutierre, as in the Southwark Playhouse (London) production of the play in March–April 1998; and surely Lope's *Peribáñez y el comendador de Ocaña* (*Peribáñez and the Knight of Ocaña*) is betrayed by a production in which the peasant kills his superior with a pitch-fork on stage, as occurred in a production of the play in translation by Cambridge University Marlowe Dramatic Society at the Cambridge Arts Theatre in March 1997. Oliver makes an interesting point about the set and costume in a production of Calderón's *La vida es sueño* (*Life is a Dream*) that he witnessed in the United States, observing that '[t]he unusual and impressive austerity of the scene and costume design helped the audience to listen to the play with redoubled intensity' ('Lope de Who?', 166). Although Oliver exaggerates the lack of action in the *comedia* in general his point here is valid—a Golden-Age audience would be used to listening, to appreciating poetry and linguistic virtuosity, to following the subtleties of the plot (as well as changes in location) through language, in a way that today is alien to us. Today our admiration is most often sought by visual special effects whilst in Spain, at least until the palace plays from the 1630s onwards, the pyrotechnics were largely verbal. Similarly costume on the *corral* stage did not just set a vague mood, it sent signals about location or time of day, about sex, social class or pretensions of a character. Props were used sparely in the *corral* and with a purpose, not as potentially distracting scene-setters.

New Historicism in particular, with its stress on politico-historical contextualization, risks converting Golden-Age dramatists into agitators, with a developed political and social conscience. The tendency to see the *comedia* as overtly critical of society, rather than simply sociological in nature in the sense employed by Pfister (*The Theory and Analysis of Drama*, 32–3) might be corrected by more of an emphasis on one common authorial intention. One aspect of the *comedia* which is often passed over is its wit, its novelty, its ingenuity. It is certainly possible that dramatists attempted to outdo each other in their choice of plot-lines, or explore issues (including feminist and class issues) to see how far they could go. For Tirso, it is a challenge to his comic virtuosity convincingly to conjure four Don Gils on stage simultaneously in *Don Gil de las calzas verdes*; for Lope it becomes a game to produce *mujeres esquivas* (unsociable women), until he arrives at the most outrageous of them, Laura of *La vengadora de las mujeres* (*The Avenger of Women*). Once a dramatic trick has proved successful it is emulated and toyed with until it becomes worn. The park scene in Lope's *La discreta enamorada* (*The Discreet Woman in Love*) in which the *gracioso* (comic servant), Hernando, dresses as a woman might be a comment on Golden-Age masculinity, but should be seen also as a variation on and revitalization of a comic theme. The expression of *ingenio* (wit) in plot, characterization and language[46] may, of course, have satirical goals, but is also often an end in itself.

All of these areas (not to mention the issues raised by the audience's reception of the *comedia* as a *part* of the afternoon's entertainment) need strengthening in teaching and research. *Comedia* scholarship would be poorer if we were to change tack and concentrate solely on performative contexts, but at the moment they are not paid the attention they deserve. We have not yet exhausted our investigation of the basic dramatic characteristics of the *comedia*: we should attempt to do so with the goal of contextualizing the genre adequately.

JONATHAN THACKER
University College London

NOTES

1. *The Golden Age Comedia: Text, Theory and Performance*, edited by Charles Ganelin and Howard Mancing (West Lafayette, IN, Purdue University Press, 1994), p. 1.
2. George Mariscal, 'An Introduction to the Ideology of Hispanism in the US and Britain' in *Conflicts of Discourse: Spanish Literature in the Golden Age*, edited by Peter W. Evans (Manchester, Manchester University Press, 1990), pp. 1–25, p. 21.
3. Miguel de Cervantes, *El ingenioso hidalgo Don Quijote de la Mancha* (Madrid, Castalia, 1982), p. 157.

4. My thanks for useful information on these matters go to Jack Sage, Victor Dixon, Julian Whicker, Esther Gómez, Paul Lewis-Smith, Melveena McKendrick, Terry Mason and in particular to Henry Ettinghausen who was kind enough to let me see part of his unpublished paper, 'Dama de Hierro vs. Siglo de Oro: ¿el ocaso del hispanismo clásico británico?', presented to the 'Conferencias Internacionales Hacia un Nuevo Humanismo' (CINHU) at the University of Córdoba in September 1997. Ettinghausen's research (on Golden-Age studies, not just *comedia* studies) provides figures which prove both an absolute and relative drop in the number of Golden-Age specialists. I should emphasize that not all of these scholars share my perception that there is a crisis in *comedia* studies, but the majority do. The views expressed in this article are, of course, my own.

5. Paul J. Smith, *Writing in the Margin: Spanish Literature of the Golden Age* (Oxford, Clarendon Press, 1988), p. 2. The development of this kind of criticism, epitomized by Parker's influential thematico-structural approach, is traced by George Mariscal, 'An Introduction', pp. 7–13.

6. Barry Jordan, *British Hispanism and the Challenge of Literary Theory* (Warminster, Aris and Phillips, 1990), p. 4.

7. This idea is also expressed by Smith (*Writing*, 7), and is noted as a current trend in US *comedia* studies by Barbara Simerka, 'Introduction', *El arte nuevo de estudiar comedias: Literary Theory and Spanish Golden Age Drama* (Lewisburg, Bucknell University Press, 1996), pp. 7–11, p. 9. The thirteen contributors to this volume all teach at North American institutions.

8. Peter W. Evans, 'Golden-Age Dramatic Criticism Now', *The Seventeenth Century*, 1 (1987), 49–53, pp. 50 and 51.

9. Elsewhere Mariscal very carefully defines the conditions under which twentieth-century theory can be applied to early-modern texts, bemoaning the frequent 'lack of theoretical clarity and intention', 'History and the Subject of the Spanish Golden Age', *The Seventeenth Century*, 4 (1989), 19–32, p. 21.

10. See especially Jordan, *British Hispanism* and Evans, 'Golden-Age Dramatic Criticism Now'.

11. On the question of 'relevance', see James A. Parr, 'An Essay on Critical Method, Applied to the *Comedia*', *Hispania*, 57 (1974), 434–44, p. 442.

12. One could not envisage the publication of a volume of theoretical essays on the *comedia* in the UK and Ireland, similar to several which have been published in the US, such as: *The Perception of Women in Spanish Theater of the Golden Age*, edited by Anita K. Stoll and Dawn L. Smith (Lewisburg, Bucknell University Press, 1991); *New Historicism and the Comedia: Poetics, Politics and Praxis*, edited by José A. Madrigal (Boulder, CO, Society of Spanish and Spanish-American Studies, 1997); *A Society on Stage: Essays on Spanish Golden Age Drama*, edited by Edward. H. Friedman, H. J. Manzari, Donald D. Miller (New Orleans, University Press of the South, 1998); and Simerka (ed.), *El arte nuevo*.

13. For example, one might question the extent to which the critic's theoretical approach trickles down to the undergraduate in the classroom. I am grateful

to the following for providing me with information about the state of *comedia* studies in North-American institutions: John J. Allen, Charles Ganelin, William Blue, Barbara Mujica, Catherine Larson.

14. However, Ettinghausen does discuss the need for strategies to help make the Golden Age viable ('rentable') ('Dama de Hierro').

15. As it did in the case of Anthony Close, 'Constructive Testimony: Patronage and Recognition in *Don Quixote*', in Evans (ed.), *Conflicts of Discourse*, pp. 69–91, p. 89. See also Evans's comments on Close's article, 'Preface', p. vii.

16. Grace M. Burton, 'Deconstruction and the *Comedia*: The Case for *Peribáñez*', in Simerka (ed.) *El arte nuevo*, pp. 21–35, p. 23.

17. Susan L. Fischer's 'Reader Response, Iser, and *La estrella de Sevilla*', in Simerka (ed.), *El arte nuevo*, pp. 86–104, is subtle and suggestive, especially in its equating of intratextual reading with our own reception of the play as readers/audience, and finds a new way of coming to a sound conclusion about the play in the suggestion that King Sancho's rule 'based as it is on the codes of individual desire ("gusto"), reflects a socio-political organization desperately in need of reform ("justo")' (p. 98). But it adds little to evidence already provided by: Ruth Lee Kennedy, '*La Estrella de Sevilla*, Reinterpreted', *Revista de Archivos, Bibliotecas y Museos* 78 (1975), 385–408; Frank P. Casa, 'The Centrality and Function of King Sancho', in *Heavenly Bodies: The Realms of 'La estrella de Sevilla'*, edited by Frederick A. De Armas (Lewisburg, Bucknell University Press, 1996), pp. 64–75; Melveena McKendrick, 'In the Wake of Machiavelli—*razón de estado*, morality and the individual', in De Armas (ed.), pp. 76–91; or J. H. Elliott, *The Count-Duke of Olivares: The Statesman in an Age of Decline* (New Haven and London, Yale University Press, 1986), p. 153.

18. See, for example, Charles Oriel, 'The Play of Presence and Absence: Writing and Supplementarity in the *comedias de privanza*', in Simerka (ed.), *El arte nuevo*, pp. 36–51 where there is some potential confusion for the reader between physical and metaphysical 'presence' (pp. 40–44).

19. See also William R. Blue, *Spanish Comedy and Historical Contexts in the 1620s* (University Park, PA, Pennsylvania State University Press, 1996), p. vii.

20. For example Catherine Larson, 'The Visible and the Hidden: Speech Act Theory and Cervantes's *El retablo de las maravillas*', in Simerka (ed.), *El arte nuevo*, pp. 52–65, especially p. 55 and p. 62, n. 3.

21. Henry W. Sullivan has an ingenious answer to this accusation in his 'Jacques Lacan and the Golden Age Drama' in Simerka (ed.), *El arte nuevo*, pp. 105–24, especially p. 123.

22. For José Antonio Maravall's broadly Marxist approach to the *comedia*, see especially his *Teatro y literatura en la sociedad barroca* (Barcelona, Editorial Crítica, 1990), and his *Culture of the Baroque: Analysis of a Historical Structure*, translated by Terry Cochran (Manchester, Manchester University Press, 1986).

23. For example, we now have accessible editions of plays by Golden-Age women writers and an assessment of their work, see especially *Women's Acts:*

Plays by Women Dramatists of Spain's Golden Age, edited by Teresa Scott Soufas (Lexington, University Press of Kentucky, 1997), and by the same author *Dramas of Distinction: A Study of Plays by Golden Age Women* (Lexington, University Press of Kentucky, 1997).

24. See especially Friedman's semiotic analysis of *El caballero de Olmedo*, 'Theater Semiotics and Lope de Vega's *El caballero de Olmedo*', in Simerka (ed.), *El arte nuevo*, pp. 66–85, and David Gitlitz, 'How to Read A *Comedia*: Branching Points in the Script of Lope's *La discreta enamorada*', *Bulletin of the Comediantes* 40 (1988), 53–65.

25. See also the letter which Parr's article induced Edward Wilson to write in *Hispania* 58 (1975), 481–2, and Parr's 'A Reply' (483–4).

26. Margaret Rich Greer, 'Constituting Community: A New Historical Perspective on the Autos of Calderón', in Madrigal (ed.), *New Historicism and the Comedia*, pp. 41–67, p. 43.

27. A. Robert Lauer, 'The Recovery of the Repressed: A Neo-Historical Reading of *Fuenteovejuna*', in Madrigal (ed.), *New Historicism and the Comedia*, pp. 15–28, p. 17.

28. See also Jack Sage, 'El auto sacramental de Calderón como "dramma regi" para el "Congreso de Europa" c. 1630–1680', in *Théâtre, Musique et Arts dans les Cours Européennes de la Renaissance et du Baroque* edited by Kazimierz Sabik (Warsaw, University of Warsaw, 1997), pp. 287–96, and Stephen Rupp, *Allegories of Kingship: Calderón and the Anti-Machiavellian Tradition* (University Park, PA, Pennsylvania State University Press, 1996).

29. Quoted in William R. Blue, 'Calderón's *Gustos y disgustos no son más que imaginación* and some remarks on New Historicism', in Madrigal (ed.), *New Historicism and the Comedia*, pp. 29–39, p. 36.

30. Greer, like Monsieur Jourdain, admits that she was doing it all along without knowing what it was called ('Constituting Community', 44). Victor Dixon makes a similar point, '[R]ecent theoretical approaches to the study of history and of literature have placed a fresh and welcome emphasis on *verdades de Pero Grullo*', 'Lope de Vega's *La dama boba* and other Comedies in their Social Context', unpublished paper read at the conference 'Reading the *Comedia* Historically: Texts in Contexts' at the Institute of Romance Studies, London, in February 1998. (I am grateful to Professor Dixon for letting me see a copy of his paper).

31. For an example of the exploration of new issues, see Greer, Lauer and Susana Hernández Araico, 'Coriolanus and Calderón's Royal Matronalia', in Madrigal (ed.), *New Historicism and the Comedia*, pp. 149–66; on New Historical socio-political approaches see Blue, *Spanish Comedy*, and especially his reservations about the 'deterministic' trap (35–8), a trap into which some of the contributors to the Madrigal volume fall.

32. 'La crítica de la comedia: estado actual de la cuestión', in *Comedias y comediantes: Estudios sobre el teatro clásico español*, edited by Manuel V. Diago y Teresa Ferrer (Valencia, Universitat de València, 1991), pp. 321–8, p. 322.

33. A. A. Parker, *The Approach to the Spanish Drama of the Golden Age* (London, The Hispanic and Luso Brazilian Councils, 1957). I have used the 1971 reprint.

34. *Don Gil of the Green Breeches* (Warminster, Aris and Phillips, 1991), p. 15.

35. See also William I. Oliver, who writes that the *comedia* has 'lost contact with the revitalizing creativity of practical theater artists', 'Lope de Who? (A Director's Do's and Don'ts, and Headaches)' in *Prologue to Performance: Spanish Classical Theater Today*, edited by Louise and Peter Fothergill-Payne (Lewisburg, Bucknell University Press, 1991), pp. 153–67, p. 164.

36. Peter Brook, *The Empty Space* (Harmondsworth, Penguin, 1990), first published 1968, pp. 12–13.

37. In this he does not differ from such theorists of drama as Manfred Pfister, *The Theory and Analysis of Drama* (Cambridge, Cambridge University Press, 1988), Keir Elam, *The Semiotics of Theatre and Drama* (London, Routledge, 1980), and Richard Hornby, *Drama, Metadrama and Perception* (Lewisburg, Bucknell University Press, 1986).

38. Brook's points on language and décor are echoed by Rafael Pérez-Sierra, responsible with Pilar Miró for producing Lope's *El perro del hortelano* for the cinema, 'Versión cinematogáfica de *El perro del hortelano*', *Lope de Vega: Comedia urbana y comedia palatina. Actas de las XVIII jornadas de teatro clásico* (Almagro, Universidad de Castilla la Mancha, 1996), pp. 107–14 (especially p. 111 and p. 113).

39. The work of John Varey and N.D. Shergold and their followers, notably John J. Allen, J. M. Ruano de la Haza and Charles Davis, has made staging a strong field of study; but as Victor Dixon admits, on tackling metre, 'we have yet to realize the full potential of the study of versification as an aid to interpretation', 'The Study of Versification as an Aid to Interpreting the *Comedia*: Another Look at Some Well-Known Plays by Lope de Vega', in Ganelin and Mancing (eds.), *The Golden Age Comedia*, pp. 384–402, p. 387: see also p. 392 for a good example of the potential of song (in *Fuente Ovejuna*).

40. *There Are No Secrets: Thoughts on Acting and Theatre* (London, Methuen, 1993), pp. 84–5.

41. See Victor Dixon, 'Introduction' to *El perro del hortelano* (London, Tamesis, 1981), p. 53. See also Dixon's 'Translating Spanish Plays for Performance: Toward a Model Approach', in Fothergill-Payne (eds.), *Prologue to Performance*, pp. 93–112.

42. Miguel de Cervantes, *El rufián dichoso. Pedro de Urdemalas* (Madrid, Cátedra, 1986), ll. 2916–17.

43. Lope de Vega, *Arte nuevo de hacer comedias* in Federico Sánchez Escribano y Alberto Porqueras Mayo, *Preceptiva dramática española del renacimiento y el barroco* (Madrid, Gredos, 1965) p. 133, ll. 305–6.

44. *Pedro de Urdemalas*, ll. 2582–91. I am grateful to Jack Sage for pointing out this example to me. For further examples in Lope's plays, see Dixon, 'The study of Versification'.

45. *Songs of Mortals, Dialogues of the Gods: Music and Theatre in Seventeenth-Century Spain* (Oxford, Clarendon Press, 1993), p. 24. Stein is hardly the first to point to the importance of music in the *comedia*, but the field needs more attention. Dixon gives examples of some of the uses of songs, see 'The Study of Versification', especially p. 392 on *Fuente Ovejuna*. See also, inter alia, by Jack Sage, 'The Function of Music in the Theatre of Calderón', in *Critical Studies of Calderón's 'Comedias'* edited by John E. Varey (London, Tamesis, 1973), pp. 209–30.

46. For a study of Tirso's 'prismatic' language, see H. W. Sullivan, *Tirso de Molina and the Drama of the Counter Reformation* (Amsterdam, Rodopi, 1981), pp. 149–68.

Male Homosexuality in Contemporary Spain: Signposts for a Sociological Analysis

This article does not attempt a history of homosexuality in Spain over the last hundred or so years, but an identification of what has made homosexuality a subject for social, political and sexological intervention. It aims to construct a historical basis from which I can understand what has been constructed as 'homosexuality' over time. In order to understand this homosexuality, or homosexualities, it is necessary to examine the processes and discourses which made all sexuality (including heterosexuality) an object of specialist intervention. None of these projects has been achieved in Hispanism to date. This, naturally, will only be a cursory introduction to such projects. In this account, compliance with as well as resistance to sexological discourses on homosexuality are considered to be crucial points of crossover enabling us to understand more fully what constituted 'homosexuality' at a particular time and place and what 'homosexuality' as a collection of sexual and social practices and discourses signified for participants and observers. Particularly, by identifying resistances to pathologising expert and popular discourses we not only offer the possibility of unmasking the operations of power in particular historical moments but can also see how power has perpetuated itself through time and how it makes itself visible in the present. One final introductory remark: in this article I do not attempt to analyse female homosexuality which has most probably a radically different history to that of male homosexuality. Clearly, a history of female homosexuality in Spain is an urgent necessity, and one which has barely been begun.

I begin my analysis in 1931, a year which saw a measured and well-argued response to *Corydon*, André Gide's evocation of virile male homosexuality by Emilio Donato in his *Homosexualismo (Frente a Gide).*[1] This short treatise, published by Morata, one of the country's leading publishers on medical and psychiatric themes, carefully weighed up arguments for and against the 'normalization' of homosexuality. Donato refuted Gide's arguments in favour of homosexuality as a desirable and morally acceptable form of love but at the same time argued against any criminalization of homosexuality, criticising explicitly in this sense the 1928 legislation under General Primo de Rivera which reintroduced punishment for male–male sexual activity.

The same year, Alvaro Retana, the aesthetic writer and gallant of the nascent fairy milieu of artistic Madrid,[2] railed against the renowned endocrinologist Gregorio Marañón, law reformer Luis Jiménez de Asúa and the writer Alfonso Hernández-Catá for their representation of the homosexual in the latter's 1929 *El ángel de Sodoma*.[3] Retana (writing under the *nom de plume* Carlos Fortuny) objected to what he thought was their lack of knowledge on the subject and Hernández-Catá's construction of the psychology of homosexuals: the novel was guilty either of 'perfecto desconocimiento psicológico' ('complete ignorance of psychology') or 'una preconcibida mala fe' ('preconceived bad faith') since 'solamente a Hernández-Catá (...) se le puede ocurrir hacernos que un hombre, al descubrir en sí tendencias homosexuales, se arroje tranquilamente al mar' ('since only Hernández-Catá [...] would think of making us believe that a man who discovers his homosexual feelings simply casts himself into the sea').[4] Against Hernández-Catá's generalizations, Retana retorted that men who liked other men just did not do that. If such a suicidal end were true, if the 'invert' chose the waves to end his days, 'estarían las regiones submarinas más frecuentadas que la Exposición de Barcelona' ('the watery regions would be more frequented than the Great Exhibition of Barcelona') (297). Furthermore, he said, some competent members of the 'third sex' with whom none of the above had spoken, those 'in the know', classed Hernández-Catá's work as shallow and hypocritical.

Other writers, such as Augusto d'Halmar, also brought to literary life (and death) different aspects of the homosexual question. In his 1924 *Pasión y Muerte del cura Deusto* d'Halmar narrates the doomed existence of the priest Deusto who falls in love with one of his altar boys.[5] When both realize the nature of their love, and the impossibility of satisfying it, the young lad runs away for a few days' oblivion with his friends. Unable to resist his desires, however, he returns, is reunited with Deusto, tries to convince him to flee with him but fails. The young man retreats to the railway station to escape from himself and from the priest, the priest follows, tries to catch up with him and is mowed down by a locomotive and killed as he crosses the tracks to find his sweetheart, so enclosing a circle associating deviant desire with death, sealed by the technological metaphor of the physical destruction of sexuality, crushed as a train hurries northwards, towards civilization and progress.

These three very different accounts offer some predictable and other rather unexpected outcomes in the articulation of male homosexual love and desire. The sheer impossibility of same-sex love is brutally displayed in d'Halmar's story, which, while fictional, would probably have captured the anguished life of many men and women in early twentieth century Spain. In contrast to negative or repressive accounts Donato's moderated counter-attack on Gide's justification of male homosexuality seems not only much more enlightened but also more progressive. The dismissal of homosexuality as a viable form of love should not entail its criminalization; quite the opposite, legal proceedings against homosexuals in Donato's eyes were as morally unacceptable as they were scientifically inappropriate. Further, within the context of the new Republic (1931–1936), in which many of the cabinet ministers were trained in new scientific approaches to education and psychiatry, 'progressive' law makers and sexologists such as Jiménez de Asúa and Marañón did not view homosexuality as punishable (this would be 'anti-scientific') but neither did they believe that it should flourish as an alternative or fulfilling form of sexuality: it had to be managed, controlled and possibly neutralized in a different way. Repression, then, in a traditional sense was not the objective of Marañón's and other sexologists' pleas on behalf of sexual minorities.[6] In contrast, a careful suggestive process by which homosexuality could be explained and, if possible, by means of eugenic and educational prevention, be eliminated from the individual and social body, was equally powerful, if not more powerful than pure repression. This shift from more overt and brutal repression to the management of homosexuality, layered in sexological discourse, constitutes a revolution in the way sexuality was referred to. I suggest in this article that in Spain one critical period in this shift corresponded to the late 1920s and 1930s.

It is difficult to assess the significance of the above scenarios, especially if they are merely viewed as examples of 'homosexuality'. Even on a terminological level, there are differences: 'inverts', 'homosexualism' and even an 'angel of Sodom' are referred to. While these terms may have denoted a broad collection of behaviours, it is necessary to analyse the differences between them and the changes in perception that they may have represented.

What is certain with regard to the three accounts related above is that they suggest a break with commonly held notions of (homo)sexual history in Spain which, as Francisco Vázquez García and Andrés Moreno Mengíbar have remarked,[7] run from a supposed starting point of repression and obscurantism engineered by conservative elements and the Catholic Church, through a gradual waning of repression coinciding with a more progressive era characterized by highly trained expert psychiatrists and sexologists in the 1930s, through the black night of Francoism, during which sexuality was allegedly not discussed or was simply repressed, emerging into the light of sexual tolerance in the transition from dictatorship to democracy. This linear approach, however, does not clarify why there existed different terminologies on same-sex sexuality, why opinions varied from group to group, and how apparently progressive treatment of the subject was perhaps as repressive as straightforward suppression. The story of ever-receding repression does not situate these remarks and attitudes in any intellectual framework or historical context. For example, it does not explain why Marañón's maintenance of strict gender divisions and differences was infused with a tangible concern over effeminate men and virile women;[8] or why the incipient sex reform movement of the late 1920s and 1930s was expressly concerned with homosexuality and the proper training of reproductive heterosexuality. Such questions are now standard in genealogical and social constructionist accounts of sexuality in the West. Often focused on sexological discourse as incitement to 'talk of sex', they have, however, placed less emphasis on the mapping of resistances to sexological categorization and how resistance to sexual management was afforded by dissenting voices. For, as a number of historians and sociologists have suggested, this calling into being of homosexuality was not an entirely unequal process.[9] The sexual monstrosities created by sexological discourse began to talk back and resist that very discourse which had named them, often in a plea which naturalized them as a legitimate part of life's variance. It is this resistance and dissidence towards expert discourses on homosexuality as immoral, abnormal, or psychologically flawed that break with a repression-based model and allow us to map contestation in a complex sexual history. Resistance is, however, harder to chart since it often leaves fewer marks, has few written sources, and is caged in by denial, fear and homophobia.

A number of methodological questions instantly emerge. Is it possible to talk of 'homosexuality' to refer to lifestyles, acts and identities forged over a period which spans perhaps more than one hundred years as though they were linked? We can point to a number of examples such as Genet's description of homosexual activity in 1930s Barcelona, or Buñuel's beating up of homosexuals in public urinals but do these activities mean anything beyond their own time reference?[10] What do they show about homosexuality in their own period? What light do my introductory scenarios shine upon contemporary developments in the identity/anti-identity debates in the 1990s? Uniting these questions is the status of the relationship between the past and the present: What does the past tell us about the present?

Mapping 'Deviant Historiography'

Research on the broad areas of the history and society of Spain has, especially in the former case, been reticent in its adoption of explicit theoretical bases. Where explicit theory is drawn upon, this has been more common in literary and film studies and in the relatively new field of Spanish Cultural Studies. Despite this, some Hispanic research tends to be performed in a context-less analysis of the 'text' in which the material and social circumstances of its production are elided (see Jonathan Thacker's arguments on Golden Age drama in this issue). Where theoretical resources are drawn upon, these are often British and American approaches or some exponents of continental philosophy. While the relevance of these theorists is rarely questioned, the possible usage of West European/American social constructionism has been critiqued, and rightly so.[11] Bearing in mind the limitations and dangers of 'importing theory' elaborated in one culture into another, here, somewhat in contrast, we draw upon a variety of sociological theories written both inside and outside of Spain. Some of these theories are useful since they have grown out of the analysis of Spanish realities, providing a contextualized and historicized account of gender, social change and the organization of sexuality over the pre-modern and modern period. In doing so, Spanish sociologists have adapted the research and insights of other continental sociologists and philosophers such as, most obviously, Michel Foucault, but also Marx, Durkheim and Elias in order to apply a genealogical method to gain insights into processes of change and discontinuity which inform past and present. In this article I use some of the insights provided in the different models suggested by sociologists such as Julia Varela, Fernando Alvarez-Uría, Francisco Vázquez García and Andrés Moreno Mengíbar. In addition, I draw on the approaches afforded by social constructionism, more recent Anglo- American 'queer theory' and the 'deviant historiography' of Jennifer Terry.[12] I am aware that there are points of antagonism between, for example, genealogy and social constructionism. However, my principal aim is not to explore these incompatibilities but rather to foreground the concerns of these different models and their use in the examination of a number of possible routes towards a history of male homosexuality in Spain.

These theories have in common a number of characteristics. In order to examine these and to set out the methods of these approaches a short excursion must be made into these authors' material. We will begin with the Madrid sociologist Julia Varela. Varela, in a series of research projects which have analysed the changing imbalance of power between the sexes from the sixteenth to the twentieth century, has discussed the genealogical method of research as having grown out the concerns of the classical sociologists of the eighteenth and nineteenth centuries.[13] Identifying Marx, Weber and Durkheim as major theorists of cultural and social change, Varela points out that these sociologists countered chronologies based on teleological reasoning and the adoption of single, unified laws of development and proposed instead of uniform laws which moved inexorably towards a self-proven end, the notion of change and of discontinuity in social relations (*Nacimiento*, 25–27). The consequences of this move were many. Significant for the purposes of this article is the opposition to the exercising of a 'global history' which sought to track down the spirit of an age or civilization, and the attempt to relate all events to a common thread in a period. Instead, these sociologists proposed 'general history', which sought to unveil the types of relations that were produced between different dispersed series of phenomena.[14] Rather than taking the subject as the starting point and viewing human consciousness as the origin of a discourse of continuity, genealogy takes into account especially power relations, forms of knowledge and their construction, and processes of individualization/subjectification. In this way, genealogy allows us to focus on the mediating activities of bio-power and disciplines, allowing us to reconstruct historically the material and symbolic processes which intersect in the formation of knowledges and their institutionalization, development and reception. Genealogy, then, affords us a relational approach to the workings of power and its inherence on the body through technical processes and discourses, constituting the field of 'sexuality' as a defining truth in individuals and as the mechanics of the population as a whole. At the heart of this approach is the attempt to show how 'la sexualidad y el cuerpo sexuado son investidos de determinadas propiedades e insertados en regímenes específicos de verdad a través conjuntamente de estrategias de poder y conocimiento' ('sexuality and the sexualized body are invested with particular properties and inserted into specific truth regimes by means of strategies of power and knowledge') (50). In this endeavour, there are no global, general strategies which regulate sexual identities in a uniform manner. There are *specific strategies* which should be analysed by means of specific research. Genealogy, therefore, in Varela's words 'trata de poner en conexión las formas de ejercicio del poder y los regímenes de saber con la cristalización de formas de subjetividad específicas' ('tries to connect the crystallization of specific subjectivities with the ways in which power and knowledge regimes are exercised') (61).

Vázquez García and Moreno Mengíbar have applied a similar approach to the study of sexual morality and knowledge in Spain from the sixteenth to the twentieth centuries. Sexuality, in line with social constructionist accounts, is historically placed and is contingent upon the material and discursive practices of the period. Sexuality is a cultural product with no trans-historical pre-ordained expression and results from a number of practices in permanent change (*Sexo y razón*, 13): 'Las prácticas, modos de hacer según reglas, conforman el *a priori*, las condiciones de posibilidad del objeto; no se trata, sin embargo, de un *a priori* transcendental, puro, universal, sino un *a priori* histórico, material y contingente, pues designa límites datables y móviles' ('Practices and ways of doing things according to rules configure what is *a priori* and condition the possibility of an object's existence. However, this is not an over-arching, universal, pure *a priori*; rather it is an *a priori* which is historical, material and contingent, since it traces concrete and mobile limits') (14). It is also a fragile cluster of phenomena: 'La sexualidad no es por tanto un fundamento sino más bien un precario objeto de época, un acontecimiento más o menos arbitrario y fortuito, una rareza histórica en torno a la cual se organizaron saberes, tipos de sujeto, toda una forma de racionalidad' ('Sexuality is not, therefore, a given but rather a precarious object in a particular time, an "event" which is more or less arbitrary and fortuitous, a historical rarity around which knowledge, types of subject, a kind of rationalization have formed') (29).

In order to avert the dangers of creating a false or generalized fictional homosexual subject, unchanged or in continuous development with other 'homosexuals' across long time periods, genealogy, in queer theorist Donna Penn's terms, seeks to trace the formation of sexually deviant subject positions.[15] Rather than focus on developed identities or self-proclaimed reflexivity, it is necessary to investigate 'regimes of the normal' and shift the lens off homosexuality alone, its discovery and formation, in order to scrutinize the 'normal', how this is constructed, and how it constructs insiders and outsiders.[16] Within the construction of the normal and the designation of outsider sexualities, other authors have emphasized the importance of resistances to those very discourses. In Terry's tracing of 'deviant subject formation', resistances are 'forged in conflict with medico-scientific discourses which pathologize homosexuality' ('Theorizing Deviant Historiography', 55). In this project, Terry's 'archivist of deviance' looks not only for how subjects are produced and policed, but how they are *resistant and excessive* to the very discourses from which they emerge (57). The notion of subjects created by and through discourse allows what Terry terms a 'diagnostics of power' (57). In this review of the movements of power we are watching out for the strategic seizure of the process of deviant subject construction by the very objects of study themselves, who, in their process of self-inquiry, are at times compliant and at times resistant to these discourses, partly within medicine, partially outside of it (59–60).

These models of analysis, by no means without limitations and problems of their own, seek to contextualize and historicize sexuality as a site for social, political, sexological discursive and material intervention, and seek to examine the creation of 'normal' sexuality and map resistances to pathologies of outsider sexualities. Below, by means of a number of examples, I attempt to apply these ideas to the cluster of concerns around male 'homosexuality' in the last one hundred or so years in Spain.

Tracing Hispanic Deviant Bodies and Desires

Varela, Vázquez García and Moreno Mengíbar all view important changes from the sixteenth century on to be contributory to the rise of the sexual subject and the modern concept of sexuality. In accordance with a Foucauldian analysis of bio-powers and disciplines, the eighteenth/ nineteenth century medicalization of the body is seen as a fundamental change. This realignment of discourses on the body within the context of the modernizing, centralizing state constituted an important shift in the designation of normal and pathological sexualities. In contrast to what took place in previous periods of history in the West, modernity was harnessed to the creation of the malleable reflexive sexual subject; the sexuality of a person became one of the major defining characteristics of his/her persona in a way that had probably not taken place before. It would seem that discourse on sexuality in Spain, and in particular the evolution of sexology, over a similar period coincided in many ways with that of other European countries.[17] What processes inhered in these sexological and medical sciences? What is certain is that these sciences cannot be seen to have a life of their own, growing independently and inexorably as European societies moved towards progress and civilization. Rather they grew inside/outside many other different series of transformations in society.

In Spain, despite the relative backwardness of science acknowledged by a number of foreign and national scientists, the eighteenth century was of great importance in the configuration of new dynamics which began to restructure scientific disciplines. Historian of science Sánchez Ron points to a number of governments in the eighteenth century, from the first government of Felipe V, which were particularly aware of the cultural and scientific lag of Spain and the need to modernize the country.[18] This century saw a number of key changes such as the reorganization of the military including the establishment of military academies in which scientific and technical subjects held priority. In addition, several Royal Colleges of Surgeons were created and the Spanish University was centralized and modernized. The changing power of the sciences can be seen in these developments. Since the riots and civil unrest in late eighteenth century Madrid, doctors were assigned major roles in the administration of the state and in public health. Their influence continued throughout the nineteenth century, a period in which diseases, especially yellow fever and cholera, served as a pretext for intensive medicalization and the increasing incursion of medicine, often under the banner of 'social hygiene', in the lives of the ordinary citizen.[19] With the centralization of the university, the creation of specialist academies, the modernization of the state and its political structures, one sees a process whereby specialist powers, knowledges and discourses secure a role of great importance in the articulation of the modern democratic, scientific state, drawing on Darwinist and sexological premises for the survival of the 'race'. In Spain, the rise of expert knowledges such as criminology, toxicology, anthropology and sexology came at a crucial time in the process of the reconfiguration of the nation expressing the anxieties thrown up by modernization, the power of working class movements, urbanization, and the need for a disciplined, appropriately sexualized population.

The variety of anxieties thrown up at the turn of the century can be analysed in what is represented in recent Hispanic history as '1898'. While the loss of the last major remnants of Empire in Spain did confirm a climate of pessimism, cultural concerns were tied up with pre-existing discourses on the degeneration of the race, the decline in sexual morality and the concern over the sexual health of the nation. These anxieties cannot be explained by recourse to '1898' as a complete explicative resource alone. Many of the concerns expressed in 1898 have their roots in the sexological, medical and centralizing discourses as well as the material changes of previous decades. Rather than seeing '1898' as a starting point for the making of the twentieth century, a pivotal point in the battle towards modernity, a genealogical approach allows us to see 1898 as yet another site where these concerns came together with particular force. Loss of Empire intensified the concerns of the hygienic enterprise of the eighteenth and nineteenth centuries and made them all the more urgent. The defeat of the archaic Spanish fleet served to link up various discourses on the efficiency of the nation, on the moral and physical degeneration of the race, the rise of major inner city problems, population displacement, working class power and battles over centralist/regionalist authority, resulting in a pressing need for a restorative, regenerative eugenic undertaking.[20]

The solution of 'regenerationism' represented the coming together of these concerns driven by a positivist approach as part of the reimagining of the nation in preparation for the Spain of the twentieth century.[21] The fact that positivist ideas came into Spanish society via the medical class channelled the attention of those concerned about the decadence of Spain towards a clinical view in which Spain was represented as an ailing body. So much can be seen in the writings of one *fin de siècle* commentator: 'La ciencia serena y fría enséñanos, en efecto, que la sociedad española tiene, como el país, las raíces óptimas; sólo que, como él también, anda dislocada, sin encaje, pervertida por una asoladora desarmonía, y con semejante desconcertado régimen no caben frutos fecundos de bien y de progreso' ('Cold, serene science shows us, in fact, that Spanish society and the country as a whole have optimum origins—the problem is that Spanish society, like the country itself, is out of step; it is racked with paralyzing disharmony, and with such a problematic regime there is no room for well-being and progress').[22] The call to science, with medicalized images, characterized the period. The sociologist José Luis Abellán has remarked: 'España, en cuanto organismo vivo, era una sociedad enferma y degenerada' ('Spain, as a living organism, was an ill or degenerate society'); the positivist doctor should adopt a scientific attitude using the three stages of clinical analysis: diagnostic, prognostic and therapeutic.[23] In this sense, Abellán argues, *regeneracionismo* adds up to more than an economic or political undertaking to become a series of medical prescriptions, which was supposed to regenerate Spain through specialized medical knowledge and the weeding out of undesirable or degenerative elements.

It is argued here that these interconnecting concerns provided a context for the rise of the sexual subject in Spain enabling hygienists and other specialists to pinpoint the individuals and the collectivities who contrasted with regulated, bourgeois, capitalist normality; criminals and sexual perverts, all of whom needed close vigilance in the form of specialized techniques.[24] Criminology and anthropology were two more currents which provided a theoretical explanation for 'atavism' and 'hereditary degeneration': for example, the theories of Lombroso on congenital political and criminal degeneration reached an enthusiastic audience in Spain, arriving at the time of great urban and rural unrest and the rise of working class movements.[25]

It is worth considering a number of these accounts in more detail. From an anthropological perspective, the Barcelona University Professor Ignacio Valentí Vivó's 1889 treatise highlighted hereditary and environmental dangers to the 'stock', called for a mandatory medical certificate of sexual performance before marriage, and pathologized 'sexual anomalies' as hereditary or environmental deviations.[26] Some of these accounts reach extraordinary diagnostic levels of lurid details, such as that of Bernaldo de Quirós and Llanas Aguilaniedo's 1901 account of the 'mala vida' in Madrid,[27] matched by a different author's volume on the same subject in Barcelona published in 1912.[28] In Quirós & Aguilaniedo's account, which appears to be based on Nicéforo and Sighele's *La mala vita a Roma* (1898), the city is presented as a dangerous magnet for all kinds of deviant activity. To prove their point, the two authors map the city of Madrid for sexual degenerates, drawing on taxonomies and aetiologies from French and Italian sources. The whole section on inverts is inserted in the chapter on prostitution, another sexual delinquency the modern state had to administrate.[29] After defining the various sorts of sexual invert and their activities, nineteen case studies were presented, all of whom had experienced some run-in with the law. Photographs of other 'uranists' are added (Quirós and Aguilaniedo, *La mala vida*, 280–1). Continuing Lombrosian measurements of criminal architecture, these case studies are a prelude to Nationalist specifications of the political and sexual deviant as identified in Civil War concentration camps and reported on by the military psychiatrist Vallejo Nágera in 1938–9,[30] and to the scientific studies on youth delinquents and homosexuality made by the broadly sympathetic Alberto García Valdés who also availed himself of photographs (in colour in this case) of his subjects in the nude, with reproductions of the genital organs for the assessment of their 'normality'.[31] An example of Quirós & Aguilaniedo's method is given below:

N° 7.—*La Paviosa*, de Cejín (Murcia), diez y ocho años, ayuda de cámara desde hace tres. Bigote y barba casi nulos y muy afeitados, cabello castaño obscuro, iris gris azulado claro, nariz ondulosa. Talla, 1,655.
(. . .)
Pecho lampiño; pene y testículos voluminosos; ano infundibuliforme y cicatrices de verrugas; juegos femeninos; masturbación desde los trece años, siguiendo á los

quince tactos mutuos; uranista activo y pasivo por lucro y placer; nunca ha
realizado el coito normal, porque ha carecido y carece de afición á las mujeres.
(N° 7.—*La Paviosa*, from Cejín (Murcia), eighteen years old, valet for past three.
Almost non-existent and cleanly shaven facial growth, dark brown hair, light
blue-grey eyes, uneven nose. Height 1 metre 65cm. Smooth chest; large penis
and testicles; infundibuliform anus [i.e. evidence of anal coitus], wart scars;
played with girls' toys; masturbated from age 13, followed by mutual caressing at
15 years; active and passive uranist for monetary gain and pleasure; has never
achieved normal coitus since he has no desire towards women') (*La mala vida*,
265–6)

By the 1920s, at the time of greater visibility of homosexuality in the
street and in the world of cabarets and bordellos,[32] psychiatrists such as
Antonio Navarro Fernández turned their sights increasingly on the
moral threat of homosexuality in Spain. It seems that in the early part of
the century, the public visibility of 'sexual inversion' took on a significance far greater than previous years. There was, naturally, disagreement
over the nature and extent of the phenomenon. While one sexologist of
the period played down the existence of 'stable forms of sexual inversion' in Spain and the extent of the phenomenon,[33] other sources were
afflicted by a kind of moral panic over the presence and visibility of inverts. Such is the case of Navarro Fernández's *Sexualidad. Revista
Ilustrada de divulgación científica de higiene social*, which appeared from
1925–8. *Sexualidad* was the first paper in Spain from a mainstream position to be devoted fully to the sexual question.[34] The review, flaunting
its modernistic stance, did not call for the repression of sexuality. Instead, it beseeched its readers as follows: 'We do not ask you to be chaste
but cautious, for the sake of better offspring' (the slogan 'casto pero
cauto' appeared on the front of practically every issue). This positive,
eugenic message encouraging normal, healthy, reproductive sexuality
tabled heterosexuality as an object of intervention, and, through its vili-
fication of deviant sexualities, including masturbation and homosexuality, drew up boundaries of the normal versus the perverse. In its avid
collection of morbid examples of stray sexual desire, *Sexualidad* saw itself as the interpreter of the times, and of the most recent scientific theories on sexuality and the codifier of an Hispanicized set of sexual
mores. In Navarro's lead article 'Depravación' of 20 December 1925,
the lack of definition between the sexes was linked to the rise of inversion and could only cause sexual immorality and depravity.[35] Feasting
on Madrid criminality, and a murder case among 'inverts', the expert
knowledge of psychiatry prosecuted its own case and enriched itself in
the process, enjoying bombastic triumphalism in its rooting out of

sexual degeneracy: 'La psicología sexual se ha enriquecido con un nuevo caso de perversión de instintos. Un nuevo ser amoral ha entrado en los humbrales [sic] del crimen desde los vericuetos de la inversión sexual' ('Sexual psychology has become enriched with another case of perversion of the instincts. A new amoral being has appeared on the criminal stage from the mire of sexual inversion') (Navarro, 'Depravación', 1). Just in case the innocent public was unaware how to identify these individuals, a run-down on their characteristics was given:

A la luz mortecina por falta de gas los veréis deambular sus trazos femeniles; la pintura del rostro, la ondulación de su pelo, su falda pantalón os dirán quién son a poco que os fijéis. Son los futuros delincuentes inhábiles para el trabajo por lo que solos o en pandilla robarán para satisfacer sus impunes apetitos. (ibid.)
(In the deathly poor illumination of insufficient gas light you will see them flaunting their female traits; the make-up on their faces, their wavy hair, their culottes will tell you what they are as soon as you see them. They are the delinquents of the future, incapable of work, who will steal alone or in groups in order to satisfy their degraded appetites)

The linkages between crime and sexual degeneration were cemented, to be partially erased during the Republic, restored under Francoism and, in the case of homosexuality, mainly discontinued in liberal democracy.

From this more overtly repressive position, Republican sexology began, through a eugenic and sexological campaign of diffusion of the basics on sex, and sex perversion, to articulate a more toned down, 'progressive' sexology which, once more through the incitement of healthy genital (hetero)sexuality, located the flaw of the homosexual in his/her constitution or environment and signalled at the same time remedies for their recuperation. Brash, 'anti-scientific' legislative attempts to crush the homosexual were rejected and made way for the incorporation of the homosexual into a modern strategy of control through discursive means, sometimes in the form of 'Question & Answer' columns in specialist reviews.[36] The homosexual in the words of one writer was now on the 'table of psychological dissection' and after this cathartic process of psychosexual readjustment, a better, more balanced man would walk away.[37]

It must be emphasized that this Enlightenment approach illuminated the most recondite aspects of 'dark love' for all to see. The purifying action of science would flush out all the putrefactant corners of the social body where the abnormal was ensconced. This was an intrusive expert knowledge which was designed to order sexuality 'democratically', but which was still capable of asserting the need for eugenic intervention into populations, guaranteeing the primacy of reproduction and the correct sexual functioning of the sexualized subject. Joaquín Noguera in 1930 had clarified the parameters of this eugenic task in a democratic context. In his *Moral, eugenesia y derecho*, Noguera justified desire and sexual pleasure as natural phenomena which had deep psycho-physiological roots: 'La Ciencia reivindica hoy a los deseos y al placer dando a conocer su verdadera naturaleza y estableciendo con exactitud su categoría' ('Science nowadays recognizes desire and pleasure, reveals their true nature and establishes exactly their different categories').[38] Positivist science would, through its constructed categories of desire, show the way towards the eugenic truth. The prerogatives of a healthy, reproductive race were paramount for the new experts of desire. The state, the author continued, was concerned about the relation between the sexes. For national defence, internal order and a sufficiently large working population, eugenics had the right recipe for social and biological action. Indissoluble marriage was declared contradictory to eugenic fitness and divorce was supported, to the horror of most Catholic commentators.[39] In another progressive turn, criminals in Noguera's account should not be sent to prison but instead to restorative *colonias*. The workings of power in this 'rehabilitative eugenics' are as clear to the eye as those more interventionist against personal and collective freedoms.

Despite the fact that the arrival of the Republic did suppose a shift in sexological discourse, this new sexology was not necessarily consistent, nor was it a fundamental break with the past. Sometimes, radical changes in attitudes were possible. The young sex reformer Hildegart Rodríguez is a case in point. In two of her publications from 1931, wildly differing attitudes towards homosexuality are encountered. In her *Sexo y amor*, she states that the new freedom (of the Republic) allowed homosexuals the right and the means to satisfy their desires with others who wished for the same, a remarkable assertion for the period.[40] This was part of the ripping down of taboos that sexology was engaged in. However, in another tract of the same year, this utopian libertarianism seems to have largely disappeared; homosexuality was now a social plague, which although it should not be repressed by legal means, was a condition requiring psychiatric treatment.[41] Such a change in a few months is significant and shows how a far more libertarian stance could be closed off as the interpretive schemas of sexology came to the fore. It also discounts the 'repressive hypothesis' of slowly thawing authoritarian attitudes towards sexuality as well as showing the lack of consistency of sexological discourse.

Discourse on sex in the Francoist period was as productive, but in a different way. Nevertheless, the continuities cannot be ignored. The programme of moralization and intervention in society during the 1930s was continued:

> no se interrumpe en la etapa franquista, aunque sin duda se transforma a través de nuevos compromisos y nuevas legitimaciones ideológicas. Tampoco implica un silencio sobre la sexualidad, aunque sí un posible cambio en los modos de enunciarla y hacerla hablar (. . .) Sexualidad y ejercicio del poder, sexología y política, lejos de ejercerse en direcciones opuestas, deben ser analizados en su mutua complementariedad. (Vázquez García & Moreno Mengíbar, *Sexo y razón*, 43)
> (it is not interrupted during the Francoist period, even though it is transformed in the light of new objectives and new ideological legitimizations. Nor does it imply silence with regards to sexuality, even though it does mean a possible change in the ways it is spoken about and made to speak (...) Sexuality and the workings of power, sexology and politics, far from operating in different directions, should be analyzed as mutually complementary.).

After his concentration camp experiments, Vallejo Nágera continued to pathologize 'abnormals' against an ideal type. Acknowledging that instincts were a fundamental innate element of people's psychic lives, his *Niños y jóvenes anormales* (1941) pathologized those children who from an early age touched their genitals as mental or psychological deficients.[42] This, no doubt, was an inherited factor, since it could be proven that at least one parent was a 'psychopath' (242). Worse still was the 'tan repugnante tendencia sexual' ('repugnant sexual tendency') of homosexuality (247) which could be prolonged from its passing phase in youth through to adulthood.

In other more crude accounts, homosexuality continued to be linked to all kinds of crime, leftism, the demise of the established order and the undermining of the ideal Hispanic type. This point of view was to be seen in the often reprinted *Sodomitas: homosexuales políticos, científicos, criminales, espías, etc.* (12th edition, 1973) by Mauricio Karl. This book, the author states, was written in order to show how dangerous the 'sodomite' was for the health of the nation. Amongst other diatribes, the book contains a critique of the 'sodomitical literature' of Marañón who attempted to show that the invert was not a pathological, ethical or psychological monster (Karl, *Sodomitas*, 91). In this way, Karl established a link between the pre-sexology categorizations of same-sex desire and the heretics, sodomites, and witches of Inquisition burnings. The homosexuals identified by the revised Vagos y Maleantes legislation of 1954 and the Ley de Peligrosidad y Rehabilitación Social of 1970 were the embodiment of late nineteenth century taxonomy.

We should not, therefore, see the Republic or Francoism as a total break from one another or from what went before but rather, at least in part, a continuity. Francoism was not some kind of 'throw back' to any previous period in time in a simple manner. It utilized expert discourses of its past and present in order to invoke a certain kind of knowledge which was part of the past it reutilized to justify its own moral and political position.

New Genealogies

The genealogical method, like its subject of inquiry, is clearly fragile. However, it does allow us to situate present day homosexuality in the context of the history of sexuality and consider homosexuality as a discursive field partly of its own making and partly not, through compliance and/or resistance to the categorizations of medicine and wider discourses. It also allows present day lesbians and gay men to situate our/themselves in past, present and contemporary developments and to acknowledge that we are shaped by the past and are constantly reworking the past which continues to shape us.[43] The genealogical approach offered by Spanish sociologists and Anglo-American theorists engaged in histories of gender and sexuality offers us the opportunity for vigilance over contemporary happenings and discourses, casting a critical eye over what has constituted the present from a detailed, patient study of the past. This discursive vigilance is enabled by the unmasking of the workings of power in specific scenarios, in which the homosexual is a configuration of past and present. Through our own resistances to the past and its uses in the present, we can form new subjectivities, new resistances and new relations between our real and invented pasts and contemporary identities.

The closer one moves towards the present day, the more difficult it becomes to assess change and continuity as the observer and interpreter are ever more implicated in the process. In this article I have discussed present forms of same-sex desire and discourse on them very little. I have not highlighted many examples of resistances to sexological categorization. But the purpose of this article was not to write a history of the homosexual past or present but rather to suggest a theoretical framework and signposts for future research on the complex of factors which enabled discourse on inversion and homosexuality in Spain. It is clear that the relationship between Retana's fairy world of the 1920s/1930s, and the queer movement in Madrid of the 1990s, for example, is still to be examined.[44] It is clear that in addition to investigating discourse on 'inversion' and 'homosexuality', other avenues such as effeminacy, differences according to region, class and family characteristics need to be explored. It is hoped that by following some of the threads discussed above, from a modest and fragile base, this article can contribute to a more historically-informed history of male (and perhaps female) homosexuality in Spain, at least over the last hundred or so years.[45]

RICHARD CLEMINSON
University of Bradford

NOTES

1. Emilo Donato, *Homosexualismo. (Frente a Gide)* (Madrid, Morata, 1931).

2. On Retana, see Pilar Pérez Sanz & Carmen Bru Ripoll, 'La Sexología en la España de los años 30. Tomo IV: Alvaro Retana "El sumo pontífice de las variedades" ', *Revista de Sexología* 40–41 (1989), 1–205.

3. A. Hernández-Catá, *El ángel de Sodoma* (Valparaíso, "El Callao", 1929). Marañón wrote the foreword and Asúa the epilogue.

4. Carlos Fortuny [Alvaro Retana], *La ola verde. Crítica frívola* (Barcelona, Ediciones Jason, 1931), p. 297.

5. For a study of d'Halmar's work, see Ramón L. Acevedo, *Augusto d'Halmar: novelista (estudio de "Pasión y muerte del cura Deusto")* (Puerto Rico, Editorial Universitaria/Universidad de Puerto Rico, 1976).

6. I wish to avoid making the direct link between sexology and (male) repression argued in a number of places, including Sheila Jeffreys, *Anticlimax: A Feminist perspective on the sexual revolution* (London, The Women's Press, 1990).

7. Francisco Vázquez García & Andrés Moreno Mengíbar, *Sexo y Razón: una genealogía de la moral sexual en España (siglos XVI–XX)* (Torrejón de Ardoz, Akal, 1997).

8. I am not necessarily suggesting that 'effeminacy' in men and 'virility' in women was tantamount to their association with active homosexuality. In an English context, effeminacy was for some time not seen as part of an identifiable homosexual character or behaviour. See Alan Sinfield, *The Wilde Century: Effeminacy, Oscar Wilde and the Queer Moment* (London, Cassell, 1994).

9. Michel Foucault, *The History of Sexuality. Volume One. An Introduction* (London, Penguin, 1990); Jonathan Dollimore, *Sexual Dissidence: Augustine to Wilde, Freud to Foucault* (Oxford, Clarendon Press, 1991).

10. Jean Genet, *The Thief's Journal*, translated by Anthony Blond (Penguin, London, 1967); Luis Buñuel, *My Last Breath*, translated by Abigail Israel (London, Vintage, 1994).
11. See Emilie L. Bergmann & Paul Julian Smith 'Introduction', in *¿Entiendes?: Queer Readings, Hispanic Writings*, edited by E. L. Bergmann and P. J. Smith (Durham & London, Duke University Press, 1995), pp. 1–14.
12. Jennifer Terry, 'Theorizing Deviant Historiography', *differences: A Journal of Feminist Cultural Studies* 3:2 (1991), 55–74.
13. Julia Varela, *Nacimiento de la mujer burguesa: el cambiante desequilibrio de poder entre los sexos* (Madrid, La Piqueta, 1997).
14. Foucault elaborates on this method in his *The Archaeology of Knowledge* (London, Routledge, 1997), translated by A. M. Sheridan Smith, French original 1969.
15. Donna Penn, 'Queer: Theorizing Politics and History', *Radical History Review* 62 (1995), 24–42.
16. Michael Warner, 'Introduction', in *Fear of a Queer Planet: Queer Politics and Social Theory*, edited by M. Warner (Minneapolis/London, University of Minnesota Press, 1993), pp. vii–xxxi, (p. xxvi).
17. Argentinian and European sexology also shared parallels. See Jorge Salessi, 'The Argentine Dissemination of Homosexuality, 1890–1914', in Bergmann & Smith (eds.), pp. 49–91.
18. José Manuel Sánchez Ron, 'Introducción', in *Ciencia y Sociedad en España. De la Ilustración a la Guerra Civil*, edited by J. M. Sánchez Ron (Madrid, CSIC, 1988), pp. 7–16 (pp. 8–9).
19. Fernando Alvarez-Uría, *Miserables y locos: medicina mental y orden social en la España del siglo XIX* (Barcelona, Tusquets, 1983). For an account of the rise of social, sexual and marriage hygiene as a prelude to sexology in Spain, see Richard M. Cleminson & Efigenio Amezúa, 'Spain: the political and social context of sex reform in the late nineteenth century and early twentieth centuries', in *Sexual Cultures in Europe, 1700–1996*, edited by Lesley Hall, Gert Hekma & Franz Eder (Manchester, Manchester University Press, forthcoming).
20. A recent account of the Disaster and its aftermath in English is Sebastian Balfour, *The End of the Spanish Empire, 1898–1923* (Oxford, Clarendon, 1997). The centenary has seen considerable production of texts in Spain, including the republication of some of the texts of the period.
21. I am drawing here on Salessi's ideas in 'The Argentine Dissemination' and, despite its concentration on a different era, *Refiguring Spain: Cinema/Media/Representation*, edited by Marsha Kinder, (Durham & London, Duke University Press, 1997). See also Carolyn P. Boyd, *Historia Patria: Politics, History, and National Identity in Spain, 1875–1975* (Princeton, Princeton University Press, 1997).
22. Ricardo Matías Picavea, *El problema nacional* (Madrid, Instituto de Estudios de Administración Local, 1979 [1899]), p. 81.

23. José Luis Abellán, *Historia del pensamiento español de Séneca a nuestros días* (Madrid, Espasa Calpe, 1996), p. 470.

24. See, for example, on the ideology of the 'defensa social', César Silió, 'El anarquismo y la defensa social', *La España Moderna*, January 1894, 141–48.

25. Luis Maristany, *El gabinete del doctor Lombroso (Delincuencia y fin de siglo en España)* (Barcelona, Anagrama, 1973).

26. Ignacio Valentí Vivó, *Tratado de antropología médica y jurídica* (Barcelona, Imprenta de Jaime Jepús Roviralta, 1889). Valentí Vivó was Professor of Legal Medicine and Toxicology.

27. C. Bernaldo de Quirós & J. Mª. Llanas Aguilaniedo, *La mala vida en Madrid. Estudio psico-sociológico con dibujos y fotograbados del natural* (Madrid, B. Rodríguez Serra, 1901).

28. Max Bembo, *La Mala Vida en Barcelona. Anormalidad, miseria y vicio* (Barcelona, Maucci, 1912).

29. A similar volume, also depicting homosexuality, was Antonio Navarro Fernández, *La Prostitución en la villa de Madrid* (Madrid, Ricardo Rojas, 1909).

30. Vallejo Nágera published his findings in *Semana Médica Española*, from 8 October 1938 to 9 November 1939.

31. Alberto García Valdés, *Historia y presente de la homosexualidad* (Madrid, Akal, 1981).

32. On the cuplé genre, cabaret and transvestism in the early twentieth century, see Pilar Pérez Sanz & Carmen Bru Ripoll, 'La Sexología en la España de los años 30. Tomo III: El cuplé: una introducción a la expresión lúdica de una erótica "ínfima" ', *Revista de Sexología* 36 (1988), pp. 1–128.

33. Quintiliano Saldaña, *Siete ensayos sobre sociología sexual* (Madrid, Compañía Ibero-Americana de Publicaciones, 1929), p. 43. Saldaña's remarks come from the first essay in the volume, on social life in Spain, and refers explicitly to the above study of Quirós & Aguilaniedo on the extent of sexual inversion in the country. The essay cited was actually written in 1914.

34. The Barcelona anarchist neo-Malthusian journal, *Salud y Fuerza* (1904–1914), was primarily devoted to birth control and sexual hygiene, attempting to link changes in sexual morality to libertarian revolution.

35. Dr. Navarro Fernández, 'Depravación', *Sexualidad* 31 (20 December 1925), 1–2. Lack of definition between the sexes is an aspect many sexologists would comment on, especially in the light of the rise of feminist movements. Luis Huerta, *Natalidad controlada. (Birth Control)* (Valencia, Cuadernos de Cultura, 1933), remarked that it was false to state that feminism 'masculinized' women; true feminism, he countered, exalted femininity and established clear differentiation between the sexes (p. 36). The new fashions of the late nineteenth and early twentieth century also provoked a number of cultural anxieties, especially where the 'new woman' ('mujer nueva') was concerned: see Teresa Bordons, 'Gender, literature and history: Spain from the turn of the century to the Second Republic', University of San Diego PhD thesis, 1993 (University Microfilms, Ann Arbor, 1994).

36. Such was the case of the libertarian *Estudios*. The anarchist doctor Félix Martí Ibáñez established such a forum in this paper in the mid-1930s. On Martí Ibáñez, see my 'Sexuality and the Revolution of Mentalities: Anarchism, Science, and Sex in the Thought of Félix Martí Ibáñez', *Anarchist Studies* 5:1 (1997), 45–58.

37. Dr. Félix Martí Ibáñez, 'Consideraciones sobre el homosexualismo', *Estudios* 145 (September 1935), 3–6.

38. Joaquín Noguera, *Moral, eugenesia y derecho* (Madrid, Morata, 1930), p. 104.

39. For an attempt to fuse a Catholic stance with the new science of eugenics, see J. Torrubiano Ripoll, *Teología y eugenesia* (Madrid, Morata, 1929). Also of interest are the debates in the 1933 eugenic conferences in *Genética, Eugenesia y Pedagogía sexual. Libro de las Primeras Jornadas Eugénicas Españolas* (two volumes), edited by Enrique Noguera & Luis Huerta (Madrid, Morata, 1934). My thanks to Efigenio Amezúa, Director of the Instituto de Sexología, Madrid, for sight of these two volumes.

40. Hildegart Rodríguez, *Sexo y amor* (Valencia, Cuadernos de Cultura XXXII, 1931), pp. 8–9.

41. Hildegart Rodríguez, *La Revolución sexual* (Valencia, Cuadernos de Cultura XLI, 1931), p. 9. The 'Cuadernos' appeared fortnightly.

42. Antonio Vallejo Nágera, *Niños y jóvenes anormales* (Madrid, Sociedad de Educación 'Atenas', 1941).

43. Scott Bravmann cites Christopher Hill to this effect in *Queer Fictions of the Past: History, culture, and difference* (Cambridge, Cambridge University Press, 1997), 28–9.

44. For a number of analyses on the meaning of 'queer' in Spain, see *Conciencia de un singular deseo: Estudios lesbianos y gays en el estado español*, edited by Xosé M. Buxán (Barcelona, Laertes, 1997).

45. The author would like to thank the editor Chris Perriam, Alberto Mira Nouselles, Adrian Young, Angel J. Gordo-López and Ian Burkitt for their assistance during the writing of this article.

'Waiting for the Earthquake': Homosexuality, Disaster Movies and the 'Message from the Other' in Juan Goytisolo's Autobiography

1. Foreword: From Sarajevo to Spanish Cultural Studies . . . and Beyond.

The idiot for whom I endeavour to formulate a theoretical point as clearly as possible is ultimately myself.

—Slavoj Žižek[1]

In winter 1997, after I had delivered a lecture on Reinaldo Arenas and Lacan at Southampton University, a colleague and friend from the English Department asked me (not without suspicion), 'how can you talk about Reinaldo Arenas's homosexuality without taking into account Cuban cultural specificity?' My answer was, 'how is it that you, in an English Department, *can* talk about Lacan? There was nothing strange or traumatic in my behaving as befits the Other and testifying to the 'specificity' of Hispanic culture (although in my case, as a Catalan, such taken-for-grantedness should in itself be carefully scrutinized), yet I violated a silent prohibition the moment I started to behave like them and talked about psychoanalysis, not 'cultural specificity'. . .

   This incident reminded me of a similar anecdote reported by Slavoj Žižek in *The Metastases of Enjoyment* (1994). After one of his lectures on Hitchcock at an American campus in 1992 during the war in ex-Yugoslavia, a member of the public indignantly asked him 'how can you talk about such a trifling subject when your ex-country is dying in flames?', to which Žižek replied, 'how is it that you in the USA *can* talk about Hitchcock?'. Žižek had been expected to testify as a 'victim' to the horrible events in his country (which, as he notes, could not but arouse feelings of 'narcissistic satisfaction' in the members of his audience, as this would have indirectly reassured them 'that they [were] alright while things [were] going badly for [him]' [*Metastases*, 1]). Yet what became unbearable was hearing him talk just like any other Anglo-American critic, about Hitchcock and not about the horrors in ex-Yugoslavia . . . To clarify his point, Žižek then goes on to denounce the media's construction of the 'Balkans' as the Other of the civilized

West during the war (the place of 'savage ethnic conflicts' with which any direct rapport or identification was effectively banned), and he concludes:

This experience of mine tells us a lot about what is really unbearable to the Western gaze . . . The unbearable is not the difference. The unbearable is the fact that in a sense *there is no difference*: there are no exotic bloodthirsty 'Balkanians' in Sarajevo [or, for that matter, no exceedingly exotic Caribbean homosexuals in Havana], just . . . citizens like us. The moment we take full note of this fact, the frontier that separates 'us' from 'them' is exposed in all its arbitrariness, and we are forced to renounce the safe distance of external observers . . . (2)[2]

Their non-peninsular origin notwithstanding, these two examples say a lot about what constitutes for me a subject worth thinking about under the general label of Spanish Cultural Studies. First of all, I should say that important and theoretically interesting though I think it is to discuss the matter of Spanish Cultural Studies today,[3] I do not particularly care what form the discipline takes, or even whether an academic field of this kind comes into being in the first place. That is because, paraphrasing the words of Fredric Jameson, I suspect that what is really important is that 'the right kind of discussion or argument [should take] place publicly'—once that is ensured, I believe Spanish Cultural Studies will have achieved its purpose regardless of the academic framework in which such a discussion is carried out.[4]

In the article that follows and indeed in much of my recent work, 'difference' in that 'bearable' sense which according to Žižek is so dear to the Western gaze is not the object of analysis. I am not concerned with a notion of 'cultural specificity' ('Cuban', 'Spanish', 'Catalan' or otherwise) which, as exemplified by the two anecdotes above, might just as easily be invoked to silence and narcissistically do away with alterity as to actually allow it to speak. Moreover, following from this, I am not directly concerned either with the cultural or the identity politics of what Jameson (who attributes such a phrase to the anti-Cultural Studies academic establishment in North-America) calls 'the new social movements'—antiracism, antisexism, antihomophobia, and so forth ('On Cultural Studies', 251). This is because, indispensable though I think it is to recognize the need to continue providing alternative histories and representational practices for marginalized agents in our contemporary societies (thereby further undoing what Cornel West calls the traditional '[white heterosexual] male cultural hegemony and homogeneity'[5]), I am infinitely more drawn to recognizing differences *within* subjects and social groups than to suppressing or 'glossing over' the recognition of such differences for the purpose of political strategy. Needless to say, my stance here is the exact opposite of typical right-wing subjectivist solipsism: it is not that I favour elite individualism against political 'commitment' as psychoanalysis is sometimes accused of doing; it is rather that it seems to me that giving up what Žižek calls the 'safe distance' from which the distinction between 'self' and 'other' ('us' and 'them', 'homosexual' and 'heterosexual', etc.) can nowadays circulate as anything *except* 'arbitrary' is one of the *most* radically political and theoretically worthwhile projects that can be undertaken.

A word on psychoanalysis. Placing an accent on the last stages of the work of Jacques Lacan, the so-called 'Slovenian Lacanian School' and its 'satellites' (Mladen Dolar, Renata Salecl, Žižek, et al.), have now been producing for some time some of the best and most original work in the contemporary non-clinical psychoanalytic field.[6] With their different philosophical and ideological-political emphases, such theorists propose a notion of subjective identity which is neither 'substantial' (essential) nor merely 'positional' (discursive). Thus, while showing (in post-structuralist fashion) that the subject is a historical and ideological construct invariably inflected by political and discursive factors such as nationality, 'race' and class, they also grant a central role to the notion of the 'Real'—the pre-discursive kernel which, according to Lacan, both resists and exceeds the Symbolic Order.[7]

Such a notion of subjectivity is the crucial line that separates my own work from 'deconstruction' or indeed from mainstream 'Cultural Studies'. For, although I would agree that the opposition between 'essence' and 'culture' is always already culturally *overdetermined* (that is to say, that no aspect can be isolated as 'pure essence'; that identity is determined by the network of social relations, and so forth[8]) this does not automatically mean, to put it in Žižek's words, that 'everything is culture'. With Lacan, I would suggest that 'essence' *qua* Real remains to be considered as 'the unfathomable X that resists cultural "gentrification" ' (Žižek 'Identity and Its Vicissitudes', 43), as that which is 'In me more than me',[9] by virtue of which I am *both* 'determined by the network of social relations' *yet simultaneously* (as Žižek points out) 'the one who determines which network of relations to others will determine me'.[10] The recognition of such a deadlock at the core of our usual, 'culturally-inscribed' subjectivities (the recognition that ultimately all discursive and ideological constructs, qua existing *in* language, will endeavour to 'gentrify' and 'patch up' a fundamental non-simbolizable 'excess' which becomes discernible through the fissures of their own formalisation[11]) is in my opinion one of the most radical contributions by Lacan to a contemporary analysis of identity, sexuality and culture which is neither politically naïve nor inattentive to the splits and antagonisms traversing the social and subjective fields.

And a word on 'popular culture'.[12] Inspired by Žižek's seminal readings of Hitchcock,[13] in what follows I tangentially use Hollywood film to exemplify (and hopefully clarify) a particularly difficult Lacanian concept before 'applying' it to Goytisolo's autobiography. The reason behind this method has to be looked for in a certain refusal on my part of any 'initiating secrecy' as regards Lacanian theory (or indeed Goytisolo's literature); that is to say they have to be looked for in the belief that one can only be sure of one's proper grasp of a particular concept if one is able to avoid the 'pseudo-psychoanalytic' and/or 'pseudo-literary' jargons and fully externalize the concept into a 'neutral', 'inherently imbecile' medium.[14] In my own case, such a medium was twofold: on the one hand, the so-called 'disaster film' in its 1970's manifestation; and on the other hand, Steven Spielberg's more recent *Schindler's List* (1993). It was one of my main concerns in writing this article to show that despite all the aspects which differentiated such popular culture products from each other and from Goytisolo's work (medium, genre, language, nationality, period, etc.), there was a basic structural feature which repeated itself in all of them: the fact that what appeared to be a particularly calamitous situation (standing for the utter alterity and inassimilability of the big Other in Lacanian terms) constituted a 'message' testifying to the truth of the subject's position. Or, in other words, the fact that they all represented identity as an absolute 'contingency' determined by the field of social relations, not by a supposed inner subjective 'core'.

Psychoanalysis is often accused of not being sufficiently aware of the cultural, historical, and class constraints of the main concepts and examples it mobilizes, and I am aware that an argument like mine could be taken as a proof rather than refutation of such an opinion. Rather than aspiring to a 'universal' status, however, my aim in the following pages is 'transnational' in the specific sense in which Bradley Epps uses this word:[15] not because such issues as 'identity' and 'homosexuality' (to mention just the ones on which my argument focuses) transcend nationality and shimmer in a universal flow, but because (though historical and determinate) such issues involve the differential relations by which subjects, ideologies and nations have meaning in the first place. The study of such differential (discursive) relations and their inscription in the Spanish cultural and political fields seems to me a valid project on which to base our particular brand of Cultural Studies. Neither to assimilate difference into the same nor to fetishize it into exotic otherness, but to potentiate an ethical and political view in which the frontier that separates 'us' from the Balkans (going back to my initial quote from Žižek) can truly start to be exposed in all its exorbitant 'arbitrariness'.

2. " 'I've Just Been to the Butcher's.'—"Sow!" '

The disorder of the world is a message testifying to the truth of the subject's position—the more this message is ignored, the more it insists and pursues its 'silent weaving.'

—Slavoj Žižek (*For They Know Not*, 72)

Aguardando el terremoto y la emergencia de una nueva moral entre sus ruinas y escombros, soportaba con creciente dificultad la obtusa ceguera de lo real a los signos agoreros del cataclismo ...
(Waiting for the earthquake and for the emergence of a new moral code from its wreckage and ruins, I endured with increasing difficulty the persistent blindness of the real to the ominous signs of cataclysm.)

—Juan Goytisolo[16]

One of Jacques Lacan's most enigmatic assertions occurs in his 1955–1956 Seminar on the Psychoses, in which he notes the apparently preposterous idea that, in speech, the subject always receives the true meaning of his/her discourse from the Other in inverted form.[17] The point is first made with regard to the analysis of a case Lacan encountered in his clinical practice, in which a paranoid woman patient confided to him the following story: one day, as she was leaving her home, she had a run-in in the hallway with an ill-mannered sort of chap, a married man characterized as 'shameful' and as 'somebody of loose morals'. On passing each other, these two had had a most peculiar verbal exchange: Lacan's patient had greeted the man with '*I've just been to the butcher's*', to which he had replied with an insult, '*Sow!*' (*Seminar III*, 47–53).

Regardless of whether '*Sow!*' was actually uttered by the man or was merely the result of the patient's paranoiac delusions, Lacan focuses on the underlying reciprocity between these two messages, interpreting the latter as a form of *projection* in which, in accordance with Freud's theory of paranoia, what had been placed outside the subject's symbolic organisation returned to her from without.[18] Thus, Lacan notes the way in which, on the one hand, '*I've just been to the butcher's*' (in French *charcutier*, who specialises in pork products) contained a veiled, unconscious allusion to '*Pig*' (this being what the patient had really wanted the man to understand), whereas '*Sow!*', on the other hand, albeit coming from her interlocutor, constituted in fact the true meaning of the woman's message *to herself*. Lacan writes:

> This is the important thing ... What does she say? She says—*I've just been to the butcher's.* Now, who has just been to the butcher's? A quartered pig ... That other to whom she is speaking, she says to him about herself—*I, the sow, have just been to the butcher's, I am already disjointed, a fragmented body*, membra disjecta, *delusional, and my world is fragmented, like me.* That's what she's saying. (*Seminar III*, 52)

As Lacan himself notes, the above episode only partially proves the point he is trying to make, for in non-delusional speech the other from whom the subject receives his true message in inverted form is in fact not the other with a small *o* ('the other'—i.e., the reality in front of us, namely the particular interlocutor who acts both as the subject's imaginary counterpart and his specular image), but 'the Other' with a capital O (i.e., the field of intersubjective relations, the alterity 'beyond all one can know' to which, according to Lacan, the subject makes itself recognized and which he himself must reciprocally recognise in his address).[19] In the above example, on the contrary, the patient's speech (which makes of her a psychotic) *excludes* this dimension of the big Other, so that what concerns her is actually said by the small other (i.e., the man she encountered in the hallway), by 'shadows of others' who, like 'puppets', can only echo the allusions contained in her own message without properly testifying to the truth of her own subjective position.[20]

Let us, however, focus on this question: what does it actually mean to say that, as Lacan puts it, the subject 'receives his true message from the Other in inverted form'? I wish for a moment to concentrate on this notion of 'the true message', of what 'true' means for Lacan. Truth (as in 'the truth about one's desire' or 'the truth of the subject's unconscious', whose articulation constitutes the main purpose of the psychoanalytic treatment) is an absolutely particular (individualized) concept in Lacan, yet one which is also radically *intersubjective*.[21] What this implies is that 'truth' is not reached in the intimacy of the subject's inner self-experience (it does not await in some pre-formed state of fullness to be 'discovered' by him or her) but results on the contrary from the way the subject's activity is inscribed in the public field of symbolic relations. Thus for instance, in the psychoanalytic situation knowledge does not pre-exist the dialectical movement of the treatment itself, but is gradually produced in the exchange with the analyst, who stands both for the position of the Other and for that of the subject's own unconscious, as other to him- or herself.[22]

Moreover, to say that the subject 'receives his true message from the Other in inverted form' means acknowledging an insurmountable gap or dislocation between, on the one hand, the subject's intentions and conscious will, and, on the other hand, his unconscious desire, which become two radically irreconcilable, ex-centric elements. As Shoshana Felman notes, the unconscious is a discourse that is 'other to itself', not in possession of itself; it is a discourse 'that no consciousness can master and that no speaking subject can assume or own' (*Jacques Lacan*, 123). Yet it is the unconscious, not the conscious, which holds the key to the truth about desire, according to Lacan. It therefore follows that the subject, to put it in Žižek's terms, is bound to *misfire* (*For They Know Not*, 71). The subject achieves the opposite of what he consciously intends: he gets tit for tat, '*Sow!*' for '*I've just been to the butcher's*'. However, and this is the originality of what Lacan teaches us, it is in what the subject 'gets' (not what he hoped to receive), in the unlooked-for results of his activity, that he must acknowledge the truth of his intention. As in the case of Lacan's paranoid patient, it is in the unexpected, apparently senseless 'reply' received from the Other that the subject must decipher, and painfully recognise, a far more accurate truth about him or herself than anything he or she might initially have hoped to get could ever convey.

Now; if there is an author in modern Spanish literature whose manifest 'intentions' (as expressed in his autobiographical, fictional and non-fictional written corpuses) seem definitely and irreversibly to have 'misfired' (in the Žižekian sense), this is Barcelona-born Castilian writer Juan Goytisolo. As Bradley Epps has recently pointed out, for all his admiration for such dissident figures as Jean Genet and Antolin Artaud, for all his furious attacks on the traditional symbols and myths of Spanish culture, and for all his claims that only a position of fertile marginality can secure the moral value of a writer's commitment to himself and his own work,[23] at least from the mid-eighties onwards the once *enfant terrible* Juan Goytisolo has himself become 'to all intents and purposes a consecrated writer, appearing to have secured a place in the Spanish pantheon which is elsewhere, in his writing, an object of derision' (Epps, *Significant Violence*, 311). Rather than remaining puzzled at the apparent paradox underlying Goytisolo's not-so-recent entry in the Spanish (and European) literary canons, however, we can go a step further, urged on by Lacanian theory, and read in the seemingly 'incongruous' response which his texts have finally obtained from the big Other of official, recognized Culture a far more accurate 'truth' about their meaning than anything they might have proclaimed at face value. In other words, Lacanian theory forces us to address the possibility that Juan Goytisolo, even in the most 'transgressive' and 'dissident' moments of his writing (or *particularly* at those moments) might always have shared a crucial common ground with that dominant ideology his texts appear most emphatically to contest, for which he would finally have been granted recognition. If, to paraphrase the famous final sentence of Lacan's *Seminar on 'The Purloined Letter'*, 'a message always arrives at its destination' (*Écrits*, 53), Goytisolo seems to have spent a large part of his career refusing to get that one particular message from the Other, one whose inverted, true form reads 'We always knew you were one of us', which has now become too obvious to be ignored, and whose acceptance must surely be as rewarding as it is painful.

Epps explicitly notes some of the ways in which Goytisolo's novels are *not* unequivocally transgressive or liberational; ways in which they also 'repeat and reinforce some of the most entrenched tactics and ideas of the dominant order' (*Significant Violence*, 9). Thus, rather than celebrating *Reivindicación del conde Don Julián* (1970), *Juan sin tierra* (1975), or *Makbara* (1979) among others, as 'progressive' plain and simple, or reading them as ethically or politically 'inadequate', Epps analyses the ambivalent ways in which such texts negotiate a position between humanism and the death of the subject, Orientalism and Western essentialism, feminism and a celebration of the phallus as 'the organ of power and pleasure' (173). His mainly post-structuralist and politically affirmative stance, however, excludes or takes little notice of the dimension of the big Other as I have been trying to describe, and particularly of the fact that it is in this dimension (the dimension of the unconscious as expressed in the text's fantasmatic mobility) where the meaning of Goytisolo's texts can still afford some great surprises.

This article is an attempt to bridge this crucial gap focusing on Goytisolo's two autobiographical volumes to date: *Coto vedado* (1985) and *En los reinos de taifa* (1986). At the point of intersection between Lacanian theory and the critique of identity to be found in Žižek and others, and focusing particularly on the narrator's uses of subjectivity and sexuality, I will attempt to show how Goytisolo's autobiography constructs its own discursive and ontological coherence in a series of interpellations in which it is the field of the big Other which contains and progressively 'reveals' to the narrator the truth of his own subjective position (a truth with which he subsequently identifies, and which therefore establishes the narrator's identity as both 'his own' and inescapably 'other').

3. Slavoj Žižek in Hollywood and Out

It is a common narrative technique of the so-called Hollywood disaster movie, from Ronald Neame's pioneering *The Poseidon Adventure* (1972) to Roger Donaldson's more recent *Dante's Peak* (1997), to alternate in the introductory sequences of the film between the familiar 'human drama' of a cluster of unrelated and unsuspecting characters and the 'silent weaving' of the imminent outbreak which is about to affect their lives. Thus we see a middle-aged couple celebrating New Year's Eve while on a boat trip to Athens, the grumpy policeman and his ex-prostitute wife (in *The Poseidon Adventure*); or the deaf-mute widow picking her children up from nursery school (in John Guillermin's *The Towering Inferno*, 1972) while in cross-cutting a very different story is simultaneously starting to develop: long establishing shots show bad weather conditions and ever larger waves threatening the ship's stability; a security monitor shows a fast advancing, still undetected fire in one of the building's empty floors . . .

There is nothing fortuitous or unmotivated in a disaster movie. We know that between what these characters are about to 'get' and their activities in the public field of social relations there is an unmistakable tit-for-tat correspondence. The children, the conscientious and brave hero, the middle-aged wife with a disabled daughter at home to take care of, will survive; on the contrary, the greedy contractor who overloaded the ship, the dishonest electrician who did not observe safety regulations, or the politician who refused to order the evacuation of the village, will perish. In other words, we have here a good example of Lacan's theory of the subject's getting its own 'message' from the Other in inverted form: what each of this characters 'gets' from the disaster, from this 'alterity beyond all [they] can know' or control which suddenly surrounds them, is the 'other' true side of their intention. The more this truth is ignored (as Žižek points out in one of my initial epigraphs), the more they refuse to acknowledge the painful, yet unquestionable 'subjective necessity' of what is coming to them (insisting, for example, that the captain's warnings are unjustified, or that the building's wiring system is perfectly safe, etc.), the more 'it' pursues its 'silent weaving' (and the more we know that tragedy is in fact just around the corner).

Let us now take another example from Hollywood: Spielberg's *Schindler's List*. At the beginning of the film, natty Oskar Schindler (played by Liam Neeson) is an opportunistic German entrepreneur willing to make quick and easy money out of war-time circumstances:

we see him pinning a swastika to his uniform, courting Nazi officials, or cynically admitting to his recently appointed Jewish bookkeeper Itzhak Stern (played by Ben Kingsley) that his own role as boss in the company he is about to start is 'presentation; not to work, not to work!'. Yet there is also another, very different story simultaneously developing here: the worsening of circumstances which is about to lead to the extermination of the Jews in occupied Poland. As shown in the montage sequence of the 1943 brutal liquidation of the Jewish ghetto in Krakow, Schindler is initially little more than a distant observer of such events. However, the more he tries to ignore what is going on, the more he refuses to 'take notice', concentrating on 'business' and moaning at Stern's demands that he buys 'yet another' Jewish worker out of the camps and into the 'safe haven' of his factory, the more the horrifying 'message' returned by social reality pursues its 'weaving' in him (and all the more sure we can be that, at some level, he has in fact already 'received' it and it is only a matter of time until he will indeed start selling all his possessions to save as many lives as he possibly can). Thus, we have here another example of the same Lacanian principle: although the subject refuses to decipher in the disorder of the world the truth of his subjective position, although he is not initially prepared to recognise himself as the 'addressee' of the apparently 'senseless' interpellation by the social network (which requires that he give up his economical priorities and become a man of virtue),[24] the 'message' (taking the form, for example, of the anonymous little girl in the pink coat capturing Schindler's attention at different points throughout the film) 'recurs' and 'insists' until enough strength is gathered by him finally to recognise in 'it' the truth of his intention.

It is against the background of such examples that I wish to start my discussion on the representation of homosexuality in *Coto vedado* and *En los reinos de taifa*. Goytisolo's autobiography is the story (in his own words) of a 'renaissance' ('mi renacimiento') (*RT,* 248) and a 'change of skin' ('mi muda de piel') (107), those of a writer who at a crucial point in his life chooses to give up the literary, political and sexual orthodoxies to which he owed his incipient popularity in the 1950s and early 1960s in order to follow, in decades to come, (what he experiences as) a more genuine, individualized and ethically valuable personal and literary path. Such a transformation affects all aspects of Goytisolo's life: as far as politics are concerned, his early Marxism and admiration for the USSR and Castroist Cuba give way as from the 1970s (partly after becoming aware of the appalling treatment to which homosexuals were subjected following the First National Congress in Havana in 1971) to the upright condemnation of all Western totalitarian regimes, fascist as well as communist; as regards his literary career, Goytisolo's pursuit of worldly recognition and his tactical defence of social realism in early novels such as *Juegos de manos* (1954) and *Duelo en el paraíso* (1955) develops in *Reivindicación del conde Don Julián* towards a new conception of literature as a 'gracia y condena' (*RT*, 103) ('grace and damnation'), one which following the example of, among others, Jean Genet, despises professionalisation and proclaims the writer's sole commitment to himself and his own work. Finally, as regards Goytisolo's sexuality, his public heterosexual persona from the 1950s and 1960s gives way to his coming out as a homosexual man at the age of thirty-four, a position which finds its ideal object of desire in Arab men, and which does not prevent him from remaining in a loving relationship with his long-time female partner Monique Lange.

Goytisolo establishes a clear cut, hierarchical opposition between he who he used to be in 'esa etapa de pose e inautenticidad' (*CV*, 117) ('that phase of posing and inauthenticity') during the 1950s and early 1960s, and the narrator of the autobiography as he conceives of himself at the time of the writing. The former Goytisolo was an 'impostor' and a 'fake', a vain and dishonest 'double' who used to run after social recognition masking 'su yo genuino inerme y agazapado' (139) ('his real defenceless and crouching self'); the latter, on the other hand, represents the writer's genuine, 'true' self, devoid of all former opportunistic concerns: somebody who has finally achieved 'la conquista de . . . mi autenticidad subjetiva'), (*RT*, 153) ('victory over . . . my own subjective authenticity') and learned 'sin las anteojeras ni prejuicios inherentes a toda ideología o sistema' (145) ('without the blinkers and prejudices which are inherent to all systems and ideologies') entirely to devote himself to 'el debate contigo y con tu verdad' (65) ('the debate with yourself and your own truth').

As noted in the final 'coming out' letter to Monique, Goytisolo's 'renaissance' goes hand in hand in the autobiography with the 'discovery' that he is 'total, definitiva, irremediablemente homosexual' (240) ('totally, definitively, irremediablely homosexual'). The term 'discovery' (Goytisolo uses the verb *descubrir*) seems here to imply the end point of some essentialist 'quest' towards what Paul Julian Smith calls a private and authentic 'corporeal identity',[25] a journey towards a pre-discursive, fully present core of subjectivity which one would only be able to access in the intimacy of one's inner self-experience (which is perfectly consistent with Goytisolo's previous references to his 'defenceless and hidden' self). It is one of the main contentions of this article, however, that even as Goytisolo's uses of subjectivity and sexuality appear to subscribe to the notion of such an essential, authentic and private (homosexual) self, homosexuality in *CV* and *RT* is in fact best understood when considered *intersubjectively*, as what Žižek, after Lacan, calls an 'inverted message from the (big) Other'. As in the above mentioned examples from Hollywood, whose different 'disasters' and changes of subjective position 'weave their way' into their main characters' lives until confrontation of (and identification with) their 'inverted truth' can no longer be avoided, the narrator's homosexuality in Goytisolo's autobiography constructs itself in a series of anti-essentialist movements (or interpellations from the Other) in which it is ultimately the field of symbolic and intersubjective relations (not the subject's inner self-experience) which ultimately 'contains', progressively 'reveals' and finally 'dictates' to him the truth of his desire.

4. 'Everybody Says I Love You': Homosexuality as a Message from the Other in Goytisolo's Autobiography.

There are two very characteristic technical features in Goytisolo's autobiography: the first one is the division of each of the text's main parts or chapters in a number of untitled and variable-length paragraphs or sections (some spanning ten to fifteen pages, others merely a few lines) whose sequential (dis)continuity is more associative than chronological. Each is broadly dedicated to the evocation of a singular event, memory or period in the narrator's life, and separated by blank spaces (what in cinematic terms would be 'fade outs') which bridge across years and locations, and so we are dealing here with something that resembles the Lacanian variable-ending psychoanalytic session. Paraphrasing Slavoj Žižek on Kievslowski's *Blue*, such 'blanks' between sections, like the analyst's gesture of signalling that the session is over, 'do not follow an externally imposed logic; they cut all of a sudden in the midst of the scene and thus act as an interpretative gesture *sui generis* by highlighting an element or association in the narrator's memory as especially significant . . .' (*Metastases*, 171).

However, it is on another well-known technical feature in Goytisolo's autobiography which I presently wish to focus, one which is symbolically and structurally more difficult to account for: the alternation (or 'cross-cutting' in cinematic terms) between the 'normal' flow of the first person biographical narrative and the recurrent emergence in the text of another, superimposed voice dislocating and disrupting such a flow, in which the narrator addresses himself in the second person. In such sections, distinctively marked by the use of italics and/or unconventional punctuation,[26] it is a different point of view that we get: not that of the 'public', apparently successful, politically committed, heterosexual Goytisolo of the diegesis, but that of his 'hidden' and most 'genuine' self, simultaneously expressing its dissatisfaction, shame, frustration and/or anger at the increasing distance separating 'him' from his public 'counterpart', and posing an unmistakable threat to the latter's narcissistic coherence. Commenting on the intersection between such two opposing voices in Goytisolo's writing, Annie Perrin interestingly distinguishes between what she calls 'heterotextuality' or a linear, conventional writing intended to capture external reality and historical 'truth' (as in the autobiography's most normative sections), and 'homotextuality', defined as a deviant, self-engendering discourse which subverts traditional narrative and epistemological paradigms (which in the autobiography is most thoroughly developed in the second-person sections).[27] Beyond the mere identification and description of these two types of alternating discourses, however, what escapes Perrin is the unmistakable symbolic reciprocity existing between the two; that is to say, the fact that if such an alternating technique is fantasmatically and libidinally at all successful in Goytisolo's writing it is because, as Lacan would put it, what she calls the 'homotext' does not just constitute the Other to the 'heterotext', but the 'heterotext' itself in its 'Otherness'—the 'heterotext' as a discourse whose repressed, true meaning is externalized and embodied in the 'homotext'.

Let us look at this question in some detail. The alternation between such opposing discourses can be best exemplified in regard to the events of Havana in 1963 described in *CV*, in which Goytisolo's communist affiliations forced him indirectly to condone the public humiliation and subsequent expulsion from the Cuban army of two young lesbians. Thus, in italics and with no full stops, the narrator writes on that occasion:

tú, yo, aquel juan goytisolo repentinamente avergonzado de su papel, del abismo insalvable abierto de pronto entre la realidad y las palabras, abrumado con los recios aplausos al impostor que había usurpado su nombre, a ese fantasma superpuesto a su yo real como un doble ... al fantoche o autómata cuya voz había dejado de representarle para representar en cambio a quienes le oprimían ... rubricador cobarde, mudo, de una sentencia dirigida a la postre contra sí mismo, contra su yo genuino inerme y agazapado: abandonar las catacumbas, emerger, respirar, escupir a la cara del otro, del doble, el fantasma (CV, 139).
(you, I, that juan goytisolo suddenly ashamed of his role, of the unbridgeable abyss opened at a stroke between reality and words, overwhelmed by the tumultuous applause for the

imposter who had usurped his name, that ghost imposed on his real self like a double . . . to the puppet or robot whose voice had ceased to represent him, and on the contrary represented his oppressors . . . the cowardly, silent legislator of a sentence directed in the end against himself, against his real unprotected crouching self: abandon the catacombs, come out, breathe, spit in the other's face, the double, the ghost)

It is now 1963 and we will still have to wait another two years for Goytisolo's 'coming out' letter to his partner Monique. However, not only do we know that such an outbreak of 'homotextuality' represents (to use Goytisolo's own words in one of my initial epigraphs) the first sign of the 'earthquake' or 'cataclysm' that is sooner or later completely to take over his life and set his 'familiar' world upside down (that the days of Goytisolo's 'public' heterosexual identity are in fact numbered, and so on), but we also know (and a self-addressed discourse by the narrator in the second person only confirms it to us) that there is an unmistakable 'subjective necessity' in this: that however long it takes for him to assume and recognise it, the 'disaster' which is silently weaving its way towards him is in fact the 'inverted' yet truer side of 'himself', of that 'puppet or robot' which his present position and activities in the public field of social relations have made of him.

Now; if Goytisolo's autobiography constitutes, in Smith's words, 'a narrative of sexual discovery' and a 'long and painful journey to homosexuality' (*Laws of Desire*, 34 and 41), it is no less true that it is in the big Other (in the field of intersubjective relations and not in the narrator's inner self-experience) where such a 'revelation' originates and is progressively disclosed to him—so much so that, paraphrasing the title of one of Woody Allen's latest productions, 'everybody says that he is a homosexual' *before* he knows it himself.

One of the first persons to 'reveal' as much to Goytisolo is his friend Mariano who, still at the University of Barcelona, told him that somebody (having noticed his literary tastes for Gide and Wilde) was spreading around 'el chisme de que [Goytisolo] era marica' ('the gossip that Goytisolo was a faggot'). Apparently, such news produced 'surprise and anxiety' to Goytisolo, who at twenty-one years of age used to feel equally indifferent towards men and women, and to whom, at least consciously, the idea of being or not being a homosexual 'had not even occurred' ('la idea de ser o no ser homosexual no se me planteaba siquiera') (*CV*, 171). Later on in the autobiography, after the narrator's move to Madrid, it is another friend, Lucho (with whom Goytisolo used to go out drinking) who shocked him with an even more disturbing 'revelation': some days after seeing the two very drunk together, a barman friend reported to Lucho that Goytisolo, under the effects of alcohol, had been behaving towards him 'de un modo extraño' ('in a strange way'). This time, Goytisolo notes, the information 'me sumió en un estado de humillación y desconcierto difíciles de explicar; lo que oscura e instintivamente temía desde que dejé de ser niño, se había producido con sobrecogedora puntualidad' (187) ('sank me into a state of humiliation and disarray that is difficult to express: what I had darkly and instinctively felt since I ceased to be a child had now occurred with alarming punctuality'). Finally, it is the Spanish Francoist police itself who give back to the narrator his own repressed subjective truth: in 1955 (ten years before Goytisolo's coming out letter and at the height of what he calls his 'empeño heterosexual' *(RT*, 215) ['heterosexual determination'] with Monique) he is told by a friend that a policeman has been making enquiries about Goytisolo's 'inclinaciones sexuales' (254).

The first person, however, to reveal to Goytisolo his own inverted 'message', the first who interpellated him as a homosexual (of sorts)—at a very early age indeed and in fairly traumatic circumstances—is his maternal grandfather, who sexually molested him as a child while they were living in the Barcelona family house in the aftermath of the Civil War. It is with the analysis of this episode that I wish to conclude.

As described in *CV*, Goytisolo's grandparents moved in with the family after their return from the village of Viladrau, where they had spent most of war. In a house already inhabited by six people, Goytisolo used to sleep in the library, where 'one night' he was secretly visited by his grandfather Ricardo. What is interesting about the depiction of the unwelcome sexual encounter which followed—at a time when, as Goytisolo puts it, 'yo no tenía la más remota idea de mi sexualidad futura' (*CV*, 105) ('I hadn't the faintest idea of my future sexual preferences')—is the way it already features a certain (mis)recognition: the Lacanian '*Che vuoi?*' which signals that an identification with the addressee of an interpellation by the Other has at some level already taken place.[28]

I wish to quote from the episode in question in *CV*: 'Cuando al cabo de unos minutos interminables,' ('When after a number of interminable minutes'), Goytisolo writes,

[el abuelo] pareció calmarse y se volvió a sentar al borde del lecho, el corazón me latía apresuradamente. ¿Qué significaba todo aquel juego? ¿Por qué, después de toquetearme, había emitido una especie de gemido? Las preguntas quedaron sin respuesta y mientras el inoportuno visitante volvía de puntillas a la habitación contigua . . ., permanecí un rato despierto, sumido en un estado de inquieta perplejidad. (*CV*, 101–102) ([my grandfather] seemed to calm down and sat down again on the edge of the bed, my heart beat rapidly. What was the meaning of all this playing around? Why did he make a kind of groaning sound after fondling me? I had no answers and while the unwelcome visitor tiptoed back to the adjacent room . . ., I lay there for a while sunk in a state of anxious confusion.)

As Žižek notes following Luis Althusser, an interpellation (the equivalent of the 'Hey, you there!' which constitutes 'me' as the addressee of an ideological mandate)[29] is a performative act which depends on the 'contingency' of a subject's finding himself at a certain place in the symbolic network, not on any inherent or pre-discursive subjective qualities: 'Whosoever find himself at [the place of the call]', Žižek writes, 'is [or "becomes"] the addressee [of the interpellation,] since the addressee is not defined by his positive qualities but by the very fact of finding himself in this place'.[30] However, according to Žižek, the process whereby one *recognises* oneself (*ergo* 'is constituted as') the subject of an interpellation (as its *addressee*) entails a transferential *misrecognition* of such a 'contingency', and its subsequent 'retroactive inversion' into a 'necessity' (*For They Know Not What*, 108)—i.e., the subject of the call cannot help but 'spontaneously' perceive that the Other has in fact 'chosen' him as its addressee, and that there must be 'some reason' for it. This is where the Lacanian '*Che vuoi?*' from the third form of the graph of desire comes in.[31] As Žižek notes, loaded with the ideological mandate to which he owes his constitution, the subject is automatically confronted with a question of the Other: 'What in me caused you (the big Other) to interpellate me?'; or: 'You are telling me that (or doing this to me), but what do you want with it, what are you aiming at?'; or more succinctly: 'Why am I what you tell me that I am?' (*Sublime Object*, 111–13).[32] Of course, such questions (and the '*Che vuoi?*' which epitomises them in Lacanese) are ultimately unanswerable: since the interpellation is 'contingent' and its character 'performative' in the first place (i.e., dependent upon the subject's position in the symbolic network and only retrospectively misrecognized as 'necessary'), there always remains a gap which no reference to 'real' causes or to the subject's 'actual' properties or capacities can ever fully account for (*Sublime Object*, 113).

Going back to Goytisolo's autobiography, we can now better understand the nature of the narrator's state of 'perplexity' after his grandfather left the library on that first night of sexual molestation. '¿Qué significaba todo aquel juego? ¿Por qué . . . había emitido una especie de gemido?', he wonders. In other words: 'What did he want?', or 'Why me?'—'*Che vuoi?*' Of course, such questions do not make the child

Goytisolo a homosexual (or more precisely, a pederast) like the grand-father, not at this stage, but they signal the fact that a certain transferen-tial 'misrecognition' has already started, that an identification with the addressee of an interpellation or 'message' by the Other (however senseless, 'disastrous' or obscure might it appear at this stage) has at some level *already* taken place. Regardless of how long it will take for him to identify with this mandate, regardless of how long its 'silent weaving' will need to go on before Goytisolo can recognise in it his true subjective position, the performative 'inversion of contingency into necessity' which marks the constitution of the narrator's 'total, de-finitive, irremediable' homosexual 'identity' has started here. That is why he asks, and why he cannot find any conclusive answers for that which is ultimately a tautology: 'Why do I have this mandate?', 'Why am I occupying this place in the symbolic network?', or 'Why am I the one who you tell me that I am?'. The only possible answer, of course, being: *'because you are a homosexual'*, a message which has just been put into circulation, yet one for which Goytisolo (along with us the readers of the autobiography) will have to wait for quite some time yet.

DAVID VILASECA
University of Southampton

NOTES

1. *The Metastases of Enjoyment: Six Essays on Woman and Causality* (London, Verso, 1994), p. 175.
2. This point deserves some further explanation. According to Žižek, the con-struction of the 'Balkans' as Other to 'civilized Europe' in the past conflict be-came noticeable in the way the media tended to emphasize those war scenes which were most dehumanizing and repulsive ('lacerated child bodies, raped women, starved prisoners' etc.) to the detriment of other types of coverage in which the residents of Sarajevo could have been presented as real possibilities of positive and direct identification for Western viewers, of which Žižek gives a number of examples.
3. See the excellent *Spanish Cultural Studies: An Introduction,* edited by Jo Labanyi and Helen Graham (Oxford, Oxford University Press, 1995).
4. See Jameson's 'On Cultural Studies', in *The Identity in Question*, edited by John Rajchman (London, Routledge, 1995); pp. 252–295 (p. 252).
5. Cornell West 'The New Cultural Politics of Difference', in Rajchman, ed., pp. 147–71 (p. 154).
6. For a general description of the Slovenian Lacanian School, see Ernesto Laclau's 'Preface' to Slavoj Žižek's *The Sublime Object of Ideology* (London, Verso, 1989), pp. x–xii. Of the books recently published in English and not

cited in this article, but directly or indirectly influenced by the School, the following are especially significant: *Radical Evil*, edited by Joan Copjec (London, Verso, 1996); Žižek, *The Indivisible Remainder: An Essay on Shelling and Related Matters* (London, Verso, 1996) and *The Plague of Fantasies* (London, Verso, 1997); and *Sic 1: Gaze and Voice as Love Objects*, edited by Žižek and Renata Salecl (London, Duke University Press, 1996).

7. See Žižek's 'Is There a Cause of the Subject?', in *Supposing the Subject*, edited by Joan Copjec (London, Verso, 1994), pp. 84–105, and 'Identity and Its Vicissitudes: Hegel's "Logic of Essence" as a Theory of Ideology', in *The Making of Political Identities*, edited by Ernesto Laclau (London, Verso, 1994), pp. 40–75; see also Mladen Dolar's 'The Phrenology of Spirit', in Copjec ed., pp. 64–83. For the Lacanian notion of the Real, see Žižek, *Sublime Object*, 55–84, and *For They Know Not What They Do: Enjoyment as a Political Factor* (London, Verso, 1991), pp. 3–66. For a critique of Žižek's use of the Real see Judith Butler's excellent 'Arguing with the Real' in *Bodies that Matter: On the Discursive Limits of 'Sex'* (New York, Routledge, 1993), pp. 187–222.

8. On this point, which has become a commonplace in post-structuralist criticism, see for example Diana Fuss's *Essentially Speaking: Feminism, Nature & Difference* (London: Routledge, 1990), pp. 2–3.

9. Lacan uses the expression 'In you more than you' as a synonym for *object a* in the concluding chapter of *The Four Fundamental Concepts of Psycho-Analysis*, edited by Jacques-Alain Miller, translated by Alan Sheridan (London, Penguin, 1979), p. 263.

10. Žižek writes: 'I am only what I am for the others, yet simultaneously I am the one who self-determines myself, that is, I am the one who determines which network of relations to others will determine me. In other words, I am determined by the network of (symbolic) relations precisely and only in so far as I, qua void of self-relating, self-determine myself this way' ('Identity and Its Visissitudes', 45).

11. See Lacan's *Le Séminaire, livre XX: Encore*, edited by Jacques-Alain Miller (Paris, Editions du Seuil, 1975), p. 85.

12. For a useful clarification of the difference between the English 'popular culture' (meaning 'mass culture') and the Spanish 'cultura popular' (meaning 'popular traditions'—as opposed to 'cultura de masas'), see Helen Graham's and Jo Labanyi's 'Culture and Modernity: The Case of Spain', in Graham & Labanyi (eds)., *Spanish Cultural Studies*, pp. 1–19 (p. 8).

13. Slavoj Žižek, *Looking Awry: An Introduction to Jacques Lacan Through Popular Culture* (London, MIT Press, 1991).

14. Applied to 'popular culture', the adjective 'imbecile' refers to what Žižek calls 'the inherent imbecility of the big Other' as epitomized in mass-culture. It is not a value judgement on the alleged aesthetic and/or intellectual 'inferiority' of 'popular culture' vis-à-vis 'high art' (*Metastases*, 175).

15. For this distinction see Bradley Epps's excellent monograph *Significant Violence: Oppression and Resistance in the Narratives of Juan Goytisolo: 1970–1990* (Oxford, Oxford University Press, 1996), p. 19.

16. *En los reinos de taifa* (Barcelona, Seix Barral, 1986), p. 46. English translation: *Realms of Strife: Memoirs of Juan Goytisolo, 1957–1982*, translated by Peter Bush (London, Quartet Books, 1990). Henceforth abbreviated to *RT.* See also the first volume of Goytisolo's autobiography, *Coto vedado* (Barcelona, Seix Barral, 1985). Henceforth abbrviated to *CV.* English translation: *Forbidden Territory. Memoirs of Juan Goytisolo, 1931–1956*, translated by Peter Bush (London, Quartet Books, 1989). All English translations quoted in the text are mine unless otherwise indicated.

17. *The Seminar of Jacques Lacan. Book III, 1955–56: The Psychoses*, edited by Jacques-Alain Miller, translated by Russell Grigg (London, Routledge, 1993), p. 49. An identical point is also made elsewhere in the Lacanian corpus: *Seminar III*, 36–37; and *Écrits* (Paris, Editions du Seuil, 1966), pp. 9 and 439.

18. The role of *projection* in paranoia was originally stressed by Freud in the Schreber paper, in which he notes: 'It was incorrect to say that the perception which was suppressed internally is projected outwards; the truth is rather, as we now see, that what was abolished internally returns from without': 'Psycho-Analytic Notes on an Autobiographical account of a Case of Paranoia', translated by James Strachey, in *The Standard Edition of the Complete Psychological Works of Sigmund Freud*, XII (London, The Hogarth Press, 1911), pp. 1–82 (p. 71).

19. See Lacan, *Le Séminaire Livre II: Le moi dans la théorie de Freud et dans la technique de la psychanalyse*, edited by Jacques-Alain Miller (Paris, Editions de Seuil, 1978), p. 276, and Dylan Evans, *An Introductory Dictionary of Lacanian Psychoanalysis* (London, Routledge, 1996), pp. 132–3. According to Lacan, the small other is simultaneously counterpart and mirror image, and it is entirely inscribed in the imaginary order. On the contrary, the big Other designates a radical alterity, an other-ness 'aimed at beyond all you can know' (*Seminar III*, 51), which transcends the illusory otherness of the imaginary because it cannot be assimilated through identification. Lacan equates this radical alterity with language and the field of social, intersubjective relations.

20. It is, therefore, the recognition of the irreducible unknowability of the (big) Other which characterises the non-delusional speech relation according to Lacan (*Seminar III*, 38), in which 'the subject receives his message from the [O]ther in an inverted form' (49). Where such recognition is excluded or foreclosed (as in the case of the psychoses), we find 'empty' speech, in which the subject is merely a 'puppet' caught up in the imaginary bond with an other 'who is [him]self', an other who merely echoes his own speech back to him (51), and can therefore never testify as to the truth of his desire (53).

21. For the notion of truth (vérité) in Lacan, see Evans's discussion of this term in *Introductory Dictionary*, 215–17.

22. See Shoshana Felman, *Jacques Lacan and the Adventure of Insight: Psychoanalysis in Contemporary Culture* (Cambridge, Mass., Harvard University Press, 1987), p. 124.
23. Goytisolo wrote in 1985: 'Hoy día, cuando la fanfarria hispana reproduce a diario las celebraciones de las patrias chicas medianas o grandes a nuestras glorias literarias y artísticas, el silencio, extrañeza y vacío que envuelven a mí y a unos cuantos, lejos de entristecerme, me convence de que el binomio fidelidad/desarraigo tocante a la lengua y país de origen es el mejor indicativo de un valor estético y moral en cuya hondura no cala por fortuna el dador de homenajes. La libertad y aislamiento serán la recompensa del creador inmerso hasta las cejas en una cultura múltiple y sin frontera ...' (*CV,* 38). ('Nowadays, when Hispanic bluster daily reproduces celebrations or our artistic and literary glories in small, medium or large regions of the land, the silence, alienation, and emptiness that envelop me and several others, far from saddening me, convinces me that the opposition loyalty/footlessness in relation to language and country of origins is the best indicator of aesthetic and moral value fortunately beyond the reach of the organiser of Homages. Freedom and isolation will be the reward of the creator immersed to his eyebrows in a multiple, frontierless culture ...'). Furthermore, in 1986: '[M]ientras [en España] el número de figurones prolifera, el de autores que tomen su trabajo a pecho ... parece en neta regresión. .... [T]oda idea o persona que triunfan corren fatalmente a su ruina' ('While [in Spain] the number of pompous celebrities proliferates, the number of authors taking their work seriously ... is clearly diminishing ... Anyone or any idea achieving public recognition rush headlong towards their ruin') (*RT,* 102).
24. For an interesting discussion on *Schindler's List* as the story of the shaping of a 'virtuous' man, particularly in connection to Hollywood stereotypes of Jewish superior intelligence, see Sander L. Gilman's *Smart Jews: The Construction of the Image of Jewish Superior Intelligence* (Lincoln, Nebraska and London, The University of Nebraska Press, 1996), pp. 191–206.
25. Paul Julian Smith, *Laws of Desire: Questions of Homosexuality in Spanish Writing and Film. 1960–1990* (Oxford, Clarendon Press, 1992), p. 34.
26. As Robert R. Ellis points out, in *CV* the second-person narrative is often in italic, although changes in the typeface, especially in *RT,* do not necessarily correspond to a change in voice: *The Hispanic Homograph: Gay Self-Representation in Contemporary Spanish Autobiography* (Urbana and Chicago, University of Illinois Press, 1997), p. 42.
27. In Perrin's own words: 'La confrontación entre la heterotextualidad, es decir, el relato lineal, simple vehículo de un mensaje, orientado hacia la reproducción de la realidad, y la homotextualidad, entendida como un escrito de desviación, fundada sobre el autoengendramiento y la autonomía del texto cara a lo real, que subvierte todas las instancias narrativas tradicionales': 'El laberinto homotextual', in *Escritos sobre Juan Goytisolo. Coloquio entorno a la*

obra de Juan Goytisolo, Almería, 1987, edited by Manuel Ruiz Lagos (Almería, Instituto de Estudios Almerienses, 1988), pp. 73–81 (p. 75).

28. As Žižek notes, after every 'quilting' of a subject by an ideological interpellation there always remains 'a certain gap, an opening ... "You're telling me that, but what do you want with it, what are you aiming at?"—"*Che vuoi?*"' *Sublime Object*, 111.

29. See Althusser's 'Ideology and Ideological State Apparatuses', in *Critical Theory Since 1965*, edited by Hazard Adams and Leroy Searle (Tallahassee, Florida State U.P, 1986), pp. 239–51 (p. 245).

30. Slavoj Žižek, *Enjoy Your Symptom: Jacques Lacan in Hollywood and Out* (London, Routledge, 1992), p. 11.

31. See 'The subversion of the subject and the dialectic of desire' in *Écrits*, 793–827.

32. See also Lacan on this point in 'Thou art the one who will follow me' (*Seminar III*, 271–84).

Taking a Leap Beyond Epistemological Boundaries: Spanish Fantasy/Science Fiction and Feminist Identity Politics

1. *Spain, Feminism, Fantasy and Science Fiction*

Post-Franco Spain has been termed the 'postmodern culture *par excellence*'.[1] During this period of rapid social and cultural change, apparently stable identities have been called into question, for example that of the originally clandestine opposition who found themselves in power for over a decade. In the 1991 Anthropos collection of essays on postmodernity edited by Gianni Vattimo et al., Iñaki Urdanibia described Spanish society as being characterized by 'la incertidumbre, el escepticismo, la diseminación, las situaciones derivantes, la discontinuidad, la fragmentación, la crisis' ('uncertainty, scepticism, dissemination, derivative situations, discontinuity, fragmentation and crisis').[2] This sense of uncertainty has also marked much recent theorizing of gender within Spain. Several articles by the philosopher Celia Amorós allude to the need to de(con)struct gender and the complexity of resignifying an identity for women.[3] The difficulty lies partly in the intermediate stage of *desidentificación* and partly in the lack of an adequate conceptual framework within which to construct a new identity (Amorós, 'El feminismo', 15). As Felicidad Orquín notes, it is much easier to reject or negate the feminine identity traditionally ascribed to women, than it is to invent models outside patriarchal culture.[4] In this article I will be focusing on femininity or identity politics for women, although other studies would suggest that multiple and often contradictory images of masculinity reveal a similar tension and instability surrounding masculine identity.[5]

By subsuming all women within the seemingly unitary term of 'Women's Identity', the differences between individual women are lost. Nonetheless, some sense of contingent collective identity is enabling or empowering for the oppositional politics of marginalized groups providing that it is recognized as provisional and politically assumed in order to give agency to a positional, contextually bound subject. Furthermore, whilst the category of Woman may be unstable, it is still the culturally dominant model and as such should be engaged in the struggle for change. This issue has been addressed by several Spanish feminist theorists such as Amelia Valcárcel who vindicates the adoption of a pragmatic 'we', whilst acknowledging its limitations, and foregrounds the individuality of women as opposed to an individualism which ultimately evades commitment.[6] Similarly, Rosa María Magda Rodríguez proposes an 'operative', as opposed to 'substantive' generic.[7] A growing body of feminist criticism in Spanish has considered the problematic relationship between on the one hand theories which, whilst facilitating the discussion of marginal discourses, posit the dissolution of the subject, and on the other feminist political activism which stresses the importance of autonomy and agency for women.[8] Narrative fiction provides a possible site for the negotiation of this apparent paradox through texts which radically situate the subject in the context of diverse social, cultural and discursive practices. By focusing on identity as discursive configuration the emphasis shifts from constructing an alternative generic outside patriarchal paradigms to deconstructing such fixed identities through a continual process of self-definition.

As indicated above, Spanish feminist theorists of the 1970s and 1980s noted the apparent difficulty in presenting alternatives to the patriarchal socio-cultural model. Much of the narrative produced by women writers in the late 1970s and early 1980s is testimonial in nature.[9] As such it is concerned with the crisis in identity politics and general questioning of values which occurred during the transition period. A speedy and concentrated political reform of women's rights during the decade prior to Spain's incorporation into the EU did not erase damaging cultural substructures which continued to affect gender relationships. Novels written by women seemed to echo the frustration felt by Spanish feminists at the gap between formal, juridical equality and these substructures. Women characters in them are often marginalized and feel different. However, whilst they clearly reject traditional role models, they do not seem capable of stepping out of established social and cultural frameworks in order to challenge the invisible patriarchy encoded therein. Regazzoni has termed them 'frontier women' (*Cuatro novelistas de hoy*, 15). In order to move beyond such limiting epistemological boundaries a leap into the imagination may help us to construct alternative paradigms for identity. Within the narrative of the 1980s and early 1990s an evolution can be traced from an experiential based literature to the deconstruction of phallocentric discourse and the creation of an alternative feminine mythopoesis.[10] I will be arguing that feminist science fiction and fantasy problematize notions of a stable, unified identity whilst attempting to articulate an emergent subjectivity through encounters with multiple social and cultural formations. The three novels that I will be analysing are *El rapto del Santo Grial* (*The Kidnapping of the Holy Grail*, 1984) by Paloma Díaz-Mas, *Temblor* (*Tremor*, 1990) by Rosa Montero and *Consecuencias naturales* (*Natural Consequences*, 1994) by Elia Barceló. These consciously engage in dialogue with both past and future to elucidate the present.

During the final years of the Franco regime in the 1970s, there was a switch to leftist and pro-democratic bias by science fiction writers who increasingly sought to distance themselves from models imported from the U.S.A.[11] The progressive political tendencies of authors became more explicit after the death of Franco and in the late 1980s/early 1990s there has been a resurgence in the genre with new collections appearing such as Ultramar, Orbis and in particular Ediciones B Nova, all of which have placed increased emphasis on publishing Spanish authors. Saiz Cidoncha concludes his study of Spanish science fiction by commenting on the ostensible depoliticization of the genre in the 1980s with the emergence of these slick new collections (*La ciencia ficción*, 510). I would argue that this is not the case with several women authors, both of science fiction and fantasy, who use the genres to examine identity politics.

In general women writers are barely referred to in Spanish studies of the genre. However, a pioneering corrective study has been carried out by Dolores Robles Moreno of the Biblioteca de Mujeres in Madrid.[12] This is a general study of the genre which also gives a bibliographical breakdown of women writers in Latin America and Spain. Perhaps the most important woman writer of the genre, indeed some would argue the best writer of the genre at present in Spain, is Elia Barceló. Unlike many of her contemporaries, she writes only science fiction and is one of the few writers to address issues of sexuality by incorporating lesbian characters. Various writers have written works questioning patriarchal social and cultural structures. For example in Teresa Inglés's 1970 play, *Complemento: Un hombre*, the Earth is run by a fierce matriarchy. A space crew of women from Earth along with their male cook arrive at a male dominated planet. They fight with the men and all the women are killed. Although the male cook is offered a chance to stay and possibly become chief of a tribe, he chooses to return to Earth, as he cannot escape his cultural conditioning.

As many feminist science fiction critics have argued, in contrast to the possibly conservative implications of looking for role models in the past, fiction situated in a speculative future may inform the present and also serve to question the fixity of past history set down within patriarchal paradigms. Perhaps the central concept informing this analysis of science fiction is Darko Suvin's famous definition of the genre as a literature of cognitive estrangement.[13] This concept of estrangement and its utility for the exploration of the construction of 'woman' on a social level is examined at length in Sarah Lefanu's discussion of feminism and science fiction.[14] For Lefanu the concept explains how science fiction may be both subversive and open-ended through a two-way process. On the one hand, by defamiliarizing the familiar it can increase awareness by making us view our own society critically and questioning what we may otherwise take for granted. Whilst on the other, by familiarizing the unfamiliar it can expand our notions of what is possible.

A similar argument can be made for the subversive function of fantasy and its symbiotic relation to the real. This forms the basis of Rosemary Jackson's analysis of the possible sociopolitical implications of fantastic literature in which she articulates the fantastic as a transgressive space where absence is made present through the recombination of the constitutive features of this world to produce something apparently unfamiliar.[15] Many science fiction critics such as Suvin have tended to label fantasy an escapist and static genre which does not have the speculative possibilities, and therefore academic credibility, of science fiction. However, such works may indeed facilitate an expansion of possibilities through the transformation of cultural myths and the exploration of what Rosa Montero has termed the shifting sands which lie below the appearance of normality.[16] As Germán Gullón states with reference to the perceived trend towards the fantastic by Spanish authors in the 1980s:

Parece una literatura de escape sin serlo, lo que pretende es encontrar o ampliar nuestro sistema de valores (éticos y perceptuales) más allá del que adoptamos para valernos en la vida cotidiana (...). Así pues esta generación intenta hacer dos cosas: reflejar la vida, el mundo, la España que les ha tocado vivir, mientras expanden sus fronteras vitales.[17]

(It seems to be an escapist literature without in fact being one, what it is aiming to do is to find or expand our value system (ethical and perceptual) beyond that which we adopt in order to cope with day to day life (...) Thus this generation is trying to do two things: reflect life, the world, the Spain in which it has fallen to them to live, whilst they expand their vital frontiers.)

The fantastic is therefore not so much an escape from reality as an examination of different facets of it. Both science fiction and fantasy may offer a narrative format which not only allows for the deconstruction of a coherent self—femininity as constructed by patriarchal, hegemonic discourse—but also the construction of a female subject outside the space bounded by that discourse.

2. Paloma Díaz-Mas

'Escribir sobre el medioeveo es sólo una forma irónica de escribir sobre la realidad'
('Writing about the medieval is just an ironic way of writing about reality').[18]

El rapto del Santo Grial can be placed within a trend in the 1980s for historical/fantastic novels in which history is used as a pretext to examine other themes. It is usually approached from an intrahistorical perspective. In other words history as viewed from an interior, personal perspective often in the form of first person or autobiographical narrative. This allows for simultaneous identification (with a first person narrator) and distanciation (due to location in the past) on the part of the reader. Thus the reader may deconstruct the present through a critical viewing of the past: 'En muchos aspectos la novela admite una lectura literaria, una lectura "real" aplicada al mundo medieval y luego una lectura perfectamente aplicable al mundo real'[19] ('in many aspects the novel admits a literary reading, a "real" reading applied to the medieval world and then a reading which is perfectly applicable to the real world').

Indeed the very power of such fiction to effect social change is bound up in the relationship between the fantastic and the real, and the reader's recognition of the conditions of the world as they know it transposed into a world which at first seems radically discontinuous from it. The current crop of historical novels in Spain often incorporate myth and legend as is obviously the case of *El rapto del Santo Grial*, a rewriting of a text which is itself a blend of history and legend, the Arthurian quest for the Grail. Díaz-Mas is a lecturer in medieval studies at the Universidad del País Vasco and this background is evident in the novel. It is a very writerly self-conscious text which sets out to re-examine certain literary genres and conventions in a parodic dialogue with the past which undermines notions of originality and authenticity. It delights in intertextual allusions to both medieval and Golden Age texts to the extent that it was once sent back from a Prize jury to which it had been submitted completely covered in red circles, presumably to indicate perceived acts of plagiarism (Diéguez, 'Entrevista',

79–80). This narrative technique echoes the medieval oral tradition of transmission of *romances* in which the key features are repetition and variation. Indeed there are many widely differing versions of the Grail myth which vary not only as to who finds it, where it is kept, what it signifies but also what it actually is.

However, Díaz-Mas is not engaging in blank parody or merely stylistic pastiche of texts from the past in which history is effaced by the interplay of intertextual references. As its title suggests, this novel sets out to puncture the mythical tradition of the idealistic Grail knight by exposing the material motivation behind supposedly spiritual, chivalric concepts such as honour. Moreover, it goes beyond the interrogation of the intertexts of the past to engage with and critique the patriarchal discourses of power, authority and violence relevant to contemporary debates such as the arms race. How does it do this? By on the one hand examining and deconstructing gender stereotypes from traditional chivalric discourse and on the other positing an alternative mythopoesis in which the emphasis is on matrilineal heritage and the female body, on resistance and revision or what one might argue is the double project of feminist identity politics.

The novel humorously parodies the masculine hero myths of Grail legend as a hundred women weavers led by Blancaniña (Whitemaiden) have escaped from the Castillo de Pésima Aventura (the Castle of Abominable Chance) with the Grail. They have it in their possession in the Castillo de Acabarás (the Castle of You Will Finish) scarcely five leagues from Arthur's court and are just waiting for one of the knights to come and collect it. However, this news throws the aged Arthur and his knights into turmoil as the Grail would usher in a time of peace, justice and goodness thereby making them redundant. They are far from the spiritual, pure knights of legend such as the chaste Sir Galahad. War is their central motivating force, not out of allegiance to the lofty, chivalresque ideals of honour but in order to gain the material benefits of power, wealth and jobs for the boys. Without the Grail to aim for, the knights are left without a metanarrative to follow and they therefore conspire to make sure that it is not recuperated as they cannot envisage an alternative narrative script. Lancelot and Perceval subvert their own quests and the duplicitous Arthur instructs the youngest knight Pelinor to ensure that none of the knights fulfil their quest. Ironically Pelinor, who actually desires the return of the Grail and chooses the olive tree, symbol of peace and wisdom as his ensign, follows Arthur's orders in an act of blind obedience to a hierarchical power system. In doing so he not only betrays his own moral principles but also causes the deaths of those he loves most. These include his beloved, the female Caballero Morado who is made a knight unbeknownst to him.

Her tale is, as Juana Amelia Hernández has pointed out, a clear parody of the ballad of the Warrior Maiden which traditionally ends in a wedding when the prince/knight discovers he is fighting a woman and falls in love.[20] The Caballero Morado, however, dies in her quest. Gawain suggests this is because she is a woman and therefore physically weak. However, the explanation would seem to lie not in her biological makeup but in her attempt to live by the alien, androcentric, linguistic code of chivalry which she fails to master. When she encounters the Caballero de la Verde Oliva (Pelinor) he insists that she identify herself by name and rank which she refuses to do. As he is bound by his code of martial values this leaves him no option but to kill her. In an attempt to save her life she recounts the ballad of the Doncella Guerrera (Warrior Maiden) and refers to herself as the Caballero de Santa Agueda in reference to a feast in which women rule for the day. However, Pelinor fails to pick up on these 'feminine' codes and they remain talking at cross purposes each misinterpreting the other's discursive practice with fatal results.

To a certain extent the Caballero Morado breaks with the traditional gender stereotypes for women within the chivalresque. She is not the patient wife or mother waiting at home as described by Arthur and both her colour (purple) and ensign (a fist within Venus' mirror) suggest links with the contemporary Spanish feminist movement. She defends her mother in court against her father's accusations and would seem to stand for what Victoria Sendón de León has termed *paidética*, a theory of ethics which categorizes the values of peace and justice, both traditionally associated with the Grail, as maternal.[21] Another possible interpretation is that she returns the Grail to its pre-Christian associations with femininity, sexuality and birth. However, these analogies, whilst reclaiming aspects of femininity which have been undervalued in patriarchal social frameworks, would seem to define difference through the very same binary categorizations they are ostensibly contesting. The ceremony of the Caballero Morado's knighthood affirms her femininity according to traditional schema in that it centres on her purity and not her heroic prowess. Rather than drawing her sword she must sheath Arthur's sword and draw blood, thereby confirming to him that she is incapable of fighting and capturing the Grail but also through the innuendo in the language used the inference is that the test is actually of her chastity. In order to become a knight she must lose her virginity to Arthur and his authority is literally inscribed in her body. As noted above by attempting to live by the phallologocentric codes of Camelot she is condemned to die in the unremitting chain of violence unleashed by Arthur. She would seem to be trapped by what Amorós has termed the two-way trap of patriarchy for women: either they demand equality on the same terms as men or affirm difference but within the terms offered by patriarchal discourse ('Feminismo', 32).

A rather more positive episode, although still somewhat ambivalent, is that which takes place in Acabarás. It provides, as Ordóñez suggests, a narrative parenthesis of sensuality and desire in this parade of exaggerated masculine violence ('Parody and Defiance', 158). The sexual subtext hinted at throughout the novel in lexically ambiguous references to Arthur's sword and Pelinor's lance and suggested in the title —*rapto* meaning rape as well as kidnapping—becomes quite explicit here. The Christian Grail is subverted and returned to pagan myth through ironic inversion as it is finally recuperated by the rustic woodsman who has overcome Lancelot inspired by tales of material wealth and beautiful maidens. It becomes a symbol of greed and lust as he sets about placing his *verga* (a term meaning both 'rod' and 'penis') at the service of all 101 maidens. Here arms and the phallus are clearly linked as symbols of masculine power and authority but this interpretation is subverted as they are placed in the service of women. The emphasis is clearly on pleasure and sensuality drawing again on pagan elements of the Grail legend and associated fertility cults in which women are depicted as being actively sexual (Ordóñez, 'Parody and Defiance', 160). In this episode several traditional chivalresque values are subverted. The rustic is also known as the Caballero de la Verde Oliva but unlike his double, Pelinor, he is not versed in the ideals of courtly love. Whilst traditional knights earn sexual favours due to their chivalric exploits, the rustic earns the ultimate chivalric spoil through his sexual prowess by satisfying each of the maidens in turn. Also, traditionally knights release maidens from enchantment whereas instead these maidens become enchanted (or rather pregnant) due to his services. If Pelinor, by following Arthur's patriarchal logic of violence and domination, can only bring death, his namesake brings life. The maidens also subvert traditional binary oppositions by actively controlling their own desire and sexual pleasure. Their captain Blancaniña instigates this by accusing the rustic of not attending to her needs, again quite unlike her namesake in the traditional 'Romance de una fatal ocasión' ('Romance of a Fatal Occasion') who in order to preserve her chastity, stabs a knight who wanted to dally with her at the foot of a green olive (Ordóñez, 'Parody and Defiance', 161–2). The maidens also succeed in recapturing the Grail where all of Arthur's knights have previously failed. However, whilst initially they would seem to be the active instigators of events, once the maidens become pregnant, they seem content to form a harem and follow the rustic's suggestion that they all marry thereby following traditional paradigms of passivity and restoring male authority through obedience to his every word.[22]

Like the Caballero Morado there is no place for these characters in a world ruled by Arthur. Furthermore in a Christian land there is no place for a polygamous rustic and 101 pregnant maidens so they set sail for the East. Although they take the Grail with them, it is absent-mindedly tossed into a bag of flour. They are not on a holy crusading mission to the Sarras of legend but presumably in search of sensual pleasures and leave behind a wasteland caused by the chain of deaths incurred in the search for the Grail. A regime of death has been installed within this patriarchal space and texts have been silenced, in particular the matrilineal discourse passed on between mothers and children, 'los libros yacerán en las bibliotecas cubiertos de polvo y las madres ya no contarán a sus hijos los cuentos antiguos en las viejas lenguas' (*RSG*, 86) (books will lie covered in dust in libraries and mothers will no longer tell their children the old tales in ancient tongues). Despite this seemingly negative outcome, the deferral of narrative closure through the voyage to the East suggests an opening out of new possibilities and alternative, ex-centric discursive practices. Through playful, parodic inversion and the transgressive force of irreverent, ironic humour patriarchal plots have been subverted and deconstructed.

3. Rosa Montero

Tembladal: terreno pantanoso, abundante en turba y cubierto de cespéd, que retiembla cuando se anda sobre él.[23]
('Tembladal': swampland, plentiful in peat and covered in grass which shakes when you walk on it).

In *Temblor*[24] the patriarchal plot of the hero myth is also clearly subverted in a reworking of the classical genre of the quest. The protagonist Agua Fría (Cold Water) does not follow the heroic paradigm of mastery through domination. Instead she collaborates with others to achieve her goals of both personal and social transformation. The setting for her quest is ostensibly a post-nuclear future which would suggest a science fiction novel. However, *Temblor* is a hybrid text which escapes easy classification. For Phyllis Zatlin it would seem to blend elements of science fiction and 'medieval' fantasy[25] whereas Davies terms it a marvellous romance.[26] However, it would seem to draw primarily on popular fantastic works such as those of Ursula Le Guin with whom Montero has expressed an affinity.[27] The very title of the novel, translated into English as 'trembling' or 'tremor', suggests the questioning of stable, fixed notions and, as with *El rapto del Santo Grial*, many articles dealing with the novel focus on its perceived postmodernity, particularly its playful intertextuality.[28] For example Franz cites an eclectic range of implicit and explicit references including *The Wizard of Oz*, *Star Wars*, *Die unendliche Geschichte*, *The Handmaid's Tale*, *The Heart of Darkness*, *Il nome della rosa*, *1984*, Wagner's Ring Cycle, Dante, Milton, the philosophy of Thomas Aquinas, Falangist rhetoric and Tibetan geography. As Stephen Hart notes, '*Temblor* seems to delight in cannibalized allusions to cultural texts whether popular or philosophical, and effects a postmodernist leveling of canonical texts'.[29]

However, whilst the novel does have postmodern features, it would seem to be attempting to trace the creation of an identity rather than its dispersal. In common with many feminist fantasy/science fiction works, *Temblor* does not confront the technological advances known as 'novum', common in much male-authored science fiction, but examines different forms of social organization and modes of thought.[30] During the quest to save her world from the mists of oblivion, Agua Fría comes into contact with various recognizable forms of social organization and ideological frameworks: authoritarian, capitalist, revolutionary and egalitarian, primitive hunter-gatherer. In all but the latter traditional sex-roles are reversed in that women are dominant or have power which nonetheless is fundamentally patriarchal in nature. In an interview given to Jochen Heymann and Montserrat Mullor-Heymann, Montero explains why she inverted the dominant male power structure in the novel:

Como a mí el sexismo, es decir el hecho de que por ser hombres o ser mujeres se nos obligue a tener un comportamiento determinado me parece ridículo y bárbaro, como es una cosa que me preocupa—cuál es la supuesta identidad que ha de tener un hombre o una mujer (...)—pues he utilizado esa inversión de papeles, simplemente para resaltar el absurdo de una sociedad sexista. (...) Yo creo que mediante esa inversión quizá se pueda analizar con más distancia el fenómeno sexista dentro de nuestra propia realidad.[31]
(Since I'm worried about sexism, that is to say the fact that, by dint of being a man or a woman, we are obliged to behave in a determined manner, seems ridiculous and barbaric to me personally—what is the supposed identity a man or woman is meant to have (...)—I've therefore used this inversion of roles, simply in order to

emphasize the absurdity of a sexist society. (. . .) I think that through this inversion, it is perhaps possible to analyse, from a more distanced position, the phenomena of sexism within our own reality.)

The inversion of sex roles thus serves to allow the reader to examine the structures of patriarchy critically by distancing them from those structures as they know them through the device of estrangement. However, it could be argued that simply reversing patterns of gender domination and inequality does not actually call into question gender categories. It is important therefore to note that the inversion in *Temblor* is not as simplistic nor as schematic as it may first appear. Characters of both sexes are ascribed both traditionally masculine and feminine qualities, for example, within the society of Magenta male characters can be violent, ambitious and lust for power, all traditionally masculine qualities, but are denied power because they are ascribed the traditionally feminine qualities of irrationality and an inability to control their emotions or desires. Thus both masculine and feminine roles are called into question as the boundaries between binary divisions are blurred. This is particularly clear in the episode involving the treacherous androgynous kalinin. For Hart this is used as evidence that the novel expresses a deep-seated fear of gender trouble (*White Ink*, 137). It is a commonplace in feminist science fiction criticism to assume that the androgyne is the perfect image of unity and harmony. However, this particular androgyne would seem to meld together negative traits which are traditionally described as both masculine and feminine. I would suggest that rather than interpreting this as an expression of anxiety towards the destabilization of gender categories, this could be seen as a critique of a common utopian scenario in speculative fiction. The alternative posited here would seem to lie in neither inverting the present patriarchal structure, nor in merging the two sides of the binary dichotomy drawn between genders but in somehow moving radically beyond current conceptions of femininity and masculinity. As Davies asserts, Montero would seem to be clearing a space between essentialist and non-essentialist positions (*Contemporary Feminist Fiction*, 160). On the one hand she seems to celebrate the power of women as mothers since Agua Fría sets out on her quest not only to save her world but to avenge the death of her birth mother; and to a certain extent the novel partakes in revisionary mythmaking with its positive valuation of female life events such as the menarche. On the other hand, the maternal figures portrayed are highly ambivalent, capable of treachery and murder to achieve their aims. Moreover, supposedly innate gender differences, such as the skills of telepathy, hypnosis and telekinesis which the priest-esses of Magenta use to control physically stronger men, are shown to be culturally constructed and transmitted through a discourse grounded in laws and prohibitions. Thus Montero would seem to be criticizing modes of social organization in which difference is codified as the basis of a hierarchical power structure.

The novel tentatively suggests that the possibilities for change lie in a balance between the individual and the collective which has been a con-cern of both Spanish feminist theorists of identity and activists working through coalition politics who privilege fluid forms of organisation ca-pable of spontaneous action. Unlike the traditional masculine heroes of chivalry, Agua Fría does not master her world through a pattern of con-quest and dominance. Her quest provides her with the individual strength to face up to her fears and cooperate with others, both men and women, to bring down the old authoritarian order. However, *Temblor* is not a utopic feminist work describing a radically egalitarian society such as those often focused on by North American science fiction critics and futurists who tend to place positive emphasis on egalitarian and ecologi-cal practice. In the dystopic world of *Temblor* these practices are shown to be of little avail if damaging cultural substructures—represented by the crystals which Agua Fría and her friends must destroy—are left in place. This would seem to echo a trend in Spanish feminist theory to question the neutrality of equality. Paradoxically the promotion of equality may serve to validate patriarchy because it assimilates the normative domi-nant model and may act to suppress diversity. In order to achieve authen-tic, as opposed to juridical, equality it is necessary to challenge the cultural paradigms which underpin society in order to radically trans-form gender categories. Despite its seemingly pessimistic conclusion, like many critical dystopias *Temblor* has a hidden utopian streak. Agua Fría decides not to join the new order which emerges after the revolu-tion. Instead she decides to carry on travelling with her as yet unborn child—and apparently reincarnated dog—and continue her search for her identity.

As in *El rapto del Santo Grial*, there is a deferral of narrative closure as Agua Fría chooses not to reintegrate herself into society and rides off into the sunset, like the archetypal outsider in twentieth-century popular culture: the cowboy. Having journeyed to the North, the tra-ditional site of knowledge, she continues her journey to the West, the traditional site of new frontiers to be broken. Perhaps this is the nature of utopia, a place always situated elsewhere. There is no elixir or quick fix for transformation of today's society. Change is a continual process and perhaps the key message of *Temblor* is the necessity for the survival of hope in the climate of *desencanto* which followed the Transition in Spain. The model for Agua Fría, and perhaps the reader too, would seem to be the determined caterpillar who, like her mother, grand-mother and great-grandmother before her, travels steadfastly up the tree trunk (*T*, 128). Through the use of fantasy Montero highlights the power of the imagination and the need to engage critically with cultural myths in order to change social structures at their deepest level.

4. Elia Barceló.

Elia Barceló, like Paloma Díaz-Mas and many other women writers who came to prominence in the 1980s, is an academic. She is a professor of Spanish literature and literary criticism in Austria. Again in *Consecuencias naturales*[32] it is evident that the author is highly conscious of the use and influence of language in conceptualising and ordering gender relations. This is emphasised through the interaction of two very different cultures with distinct forms of social organisation: Earth and the Xhroll, aliens with humanoid features. Each is fascinated with the other's language and how that language causes them to perceive their experiences. Much as in *Temblor* the emphasis is not technological advances, although the world here is clearly futuristic with the action taking place in outer space. The description on the flyleaf of the novel makes the focus on gender explicit:

> *Consecuencias naturales* es una metáfora extensa que, narrada en tono ligero, nos transporta entre malentendidos por un paisaje de roles sexuales, clichés lingüísticos, mentiras, verdades, machos y hembras, humanos y extraterrestres, en un texto divertido y ameno que nos hace mirarnos en un espejo invertido para reírnos de lo que vemos.
>
> (*Natural consequences* is an extended metaphor which, narrated in a light tone, transports us via misunderstandings through a landscape of sexual roles, linguistic cliches, lies, truths, men and women, earthlings and extraterrestrials, in an enter-taining and readable text which forces us to look at ourselves in an inverted mirror and laugh at what we see.)

The reader is clearly being invited to view the present critically through a speculative projection into a future in which space stations are com-mon and there is ostensibly complete equality between the sexes. This equality is codified linguistically by the avoidance of a masculine generic to refer to both genders in an arrival speech by travellers in

honour of the Xhroll in which the feminine form of the nouns and pro-
nouns precedes the masculine in a form of positive affirmation to
compensate for centuries of discrimination (*CN*, 16). As will become
evident, however, the rules and regulations in place to promote equality have not been sufficient to completely erase discriminatory
behaviour. The persistence of traditional gender stereotypes is manifest
in the attitudes of many of the male members of the crew of the space
station Victoria who outnumber their female counterparts by three to
one. Indeed, the clearest example of this is the cocksure lieutenant
Nico Andrade who is the main human male protagonist. He conceives
of women as purely sexual objects and is determined to add the first
physical contact with a Xhroll to his string of conquests. He deceives
the Xhroll he has intercourse with into thinking that he has taken con-
traceptive precautions when in fact he has swallowed an aspirin.
Consequently he is described by Kaminsky, the commander of the
Victoria, as being of:

una mentalidad de macho antediluviano que creíamos desaparecido para siempre
después de tantos siglos de lucha de por la igualdad de los sexos (*CN*, 48).
(the mentality of an antediluvian chauvinist which we thought had disappeared
forever after so many centuries of struggle for equality between the sexes.)

The present is explicitly criticised from the future perspective of characters such as Kaminsky and Colonel Diana Ortega who are horrified
by Andrade's seemingly anachronistic behaviour. Ironically, the natural
consequences of Andrade's deception are that he, and not the Xhroll,
becomes pregnant. The interpenetration of boundaries between a human and alien other breaks down clearcut assumptions about what is
natural and confounds fixed sexual divisions.

Central Earth Government accedes to the Xhroll request that
Andrade travel to Xhroll to give birth provided that he is accompanied
by Captain Charlie Fonseca of the intelligence service. Fonseca, along
with the Xhroll Ankhjaia'langtxhrl, provides the reader with a first-
person commentary on the social and cultural differences between
their respective worlds in the form of sections of interior monologue
which are interspersed within the third person narrative. The focus in
these sections is on language, sexuality and maternity which are con-
ceptualised in a distinct manner in each culture. Ankhjaia'langtxhrl is
particularly fascinated by the gendering of all things through binary
division in terrestrial language.

Cristina Brullet Tenas has traced how sex and gender roles have been
conflated in patriarchal society through the association of the female

capacity to give birth with the social role of mothering.[33] This seem-ingly natural division, or biological fallacy, is called into question by the Xhroll who cannot be easily categorised as either masculine or feminine. Ankhjaia'langtxhrl in appearance is a 'she' and yet it is Ankhjaia'langtxhrl who impregnates Andrade suggesting that this 'she' is thereby a 'he'. Furthermore, seemingly indissoluble links between sex and gender break down with Andrade's pregnancy. On Xhroll he is conceived of as an 'abba' or mother and as such his movements, free-dom of speech and action are severely constrained. This is partly because the Xhroll are on the verge of extinction and therefore endeavour to protect their 'hol'la' (child) as much as possible. However, it is also because 'abba' are regarded as being completely dependent on their 'ari-arkjh' (protectors). In a reversal of conven-tional patriarchal parenting roles, Nico is the supposedly passive 'abba', a role he has great difficult adjusting to, and Charlie, a woman, is the active 'ari-arkjh'. These two social roles would seem to take traditional binary divisions to the extreme, using exaggeration, as in *El rapto del Santo Grial*, to provoke the reader into critiquing of such hierarchical paradigms.

However, the gendering of the Xhroll is not binary, as it first may ap-pear. A third position exists, that of the xhrea who are deemed as having neither the capacity to impregnate nor to bear children. It is they who actually control Xhroll, as they are seen to act free of damaging hor-monal impulses. The final twist in this tale comes when Nico manages to impregnate a xhrea, thereby demonstrating that the sexual and social roles of the 'abba', 'ari-arkjh' and 'xhrea' are not natural and cannot be essentialized as such. As the narrative concludes, the now pregnant xhrea, Hithrolgh, realises that becoming an 'abba' implies an inacceptable change of status and asks Fonseca for advice as Earth would seem to have, in theory at least, a more egalitarian society. The constructed nature of 'gender' in both societies is evident to the reader and acutely observed by the intelligence officer Charlie Fonseca, whose name is appropriately neither masculine nor feminine. As Fonseca con-cludes, after contact with the Xhroll, simple binary divisions of both sex and gender break down. With regard to the 'hol'la', Lenny, it is not evi-dent whether it is her daughter or son or whether she is now to be regarded as a mother or father:

Al fin y al cabo era su hija.
O su hijo.
Y ella era su madre.

O su padre.
O su madre.
O su padre. O . . . (*CN*, 185)

(After all she was her daughter.
Or her son.
And she was his/her mother.
Or her/his father.
Or his/her mother.
Or her/his father. Or . . .)

In this humourous text then, linguistic cliches and gender stereotypes are deconstructed through the device of estrangement on many levels: temporal through location in the future, geographical and cultural through the encounter with the Xhroll and biological through a male pregnancy.

5. Conclusion. Never-Ending Story

All of the novels discussed above are situated outside contemporary patriarchal socio-cultural structures in fantasy worlds that allow readers to distance themselves from those structures in order to examine them critically. Through intertextual reference, ironic inversion and parody they break down the boundaries between popular culture and high art in order to further engage the reader whilst questioning what has been legitimized by particular cultural forms of expression. Far from being 'merely escapist' they effect a postmodern critique of identity and subjectivity in order to deconstruct certainties and fixed notions of gender by focusing on the partiality of knowledge and the limitations of patriarchal discursive constructs to conceptualize gender relationships. Whilst they may certainly be described as postmodernly playful texts, they explicitly engage in the critical deconstruction of hierarchical power relations thereby avoiding what Helen Graham and Jo Labanyi have described as the possible conservative implications of ironic postmodern posturing which ultimately disguises the hierarchical relationships between participating cultures.[34] There is an acute awareness of the use of language within particular historical, social and cultural frameworks as these texts engage with the often paradoxical rhetoric of rupture that categorizes much postmodernist thinking. In other words they use and subvert the concepts of gender which they challenge in order to move towards a notion of shifting and positional identity which is constantly being reinvented and rewritten. I would argue that these texts confound the divisions drawn up by many critics between Spanish women writers who are categorised as either opting for the modernist project of an authentic (feminine) self or, as posited by Labanyi, the postmodern play of unstable identity with no regard to gender issues.[35] Instead, these texts would seem to move towards what Rodríguez Magda has termed a transmodern feminism which combines the postmodern interrogation of fixed positions with an emancipatory, critical theory of agency ('Por un feminismo transmoderno', 312).

VANESSA KNIGHTS
University of Newcastle

NOTES

1. Jo Labanyi, 'Postmodernism, Pastiche and the Problem of Cultural Identity', talk given at the Instituto Cervantes, London in the cycle 'La cultura española en su contexto europeo' on 7 June 1993.

2. Iñaki Urdanibia, 'Lo narrativo en la posmodernidad', in *En torno a la posmodernidad*, edited by Gianni Vattimo et al. (Barcelona, Anthropos, 1991), pp. 41–75, (pp. 68–9)

3. Celia Amorós, 'Feminismo: Discurso de la diferencia, discurso de la igualdad', *El Viejo Topo* extra 10 (1980), 30–3; 'El feminismo entre la autonomía y los partidos', *Zona Abierta* 23 (1980), 118–25; 'Espacio de los iguales, espacio de las idénticas: Notas sobre el poder y el principio de individuación', *Arbor* 504 (1987), 123–5; 'Del feminismo al feminismo', *Debats*, 27 (1989), 52–60; 'El feminismo como axis emancipatoria', *Canelobre* 23–24 (1992), 15–27.

4. Felicidad Orquín, 'De las mujeres que escriben, lo femenino y el modelo imposible', *Langaiak* 6 (1984), 31–7 (31).

5. Instituto de la Mujer, *Los hombres españoles* (Madrid, Instituto de la Mujer and Ministerio de Asuntos Sociales, 1988); Félix Ortega et al., *La flotante identidad sexual: La construcción del género en la vida cotidiana de la juventud* (Madrid, Universidad Complutense and Comunidad de Madrid, Dirección General de la Mujer, 1993).

6. Amelia Valcárcel, *Sexo y filosofía: Sobre «mujer y poder»* (Barcelona, Anthropos, 1991), pp. 71–87.

7. Rosa María Rodríguez Magda, 'De la modernidad olvidadiza a la usurpación postmoderna', *Canelobre* 23–24 (1992), 53–63 (58).

8. Concha Fagoaga, 'Prácticas de la posmodernidad', in *Encuentros sobre modernidad y postmodernidad (1987, Madrid)* edited by Pedro Castrortega et al, (Madrid, Fundación de Investigaciones Marxistas, 1989), pp. 185–8; Cristina Molina Petit, 'Lo femenino como metáfora en la racionalidad post-moderna y su (escasa) utilidad para la Teoría Feminista', *Isegoría: Revista de Filosofía*

Moral y Política 6 (1992), 129–43; Rosa María Rodríguez Magda, 'Por un feminismo transmoderno', in *Juntas y a por Todas: Jornadas Feministas* edited by Federación de Organizaciones Feministas del Estado Español (Madrid, Comunidad de Madrid, Dirección General de la Mujer, 1994), pp. 303–12; and 'De la modernidad olvidadiza'.

9. See Susanna Regazzoni, *Cuatro novelistas de hoy: Estudio y entrevistas* (Milan, Cisalpino-Goliardica, 1984); Isabel Romero et al., 'Feminismo y literatura: la narrativa de los años 70', in *Literatura y vida cotidiana: Actas de las cuartas jornadas de investigación interdisciplinaria del Seminario de Estudios de la Mujer de la Universidad Autónoma de Madrid* edited by María Angeles Durán and José Antonio Rey (Zaragoza, Prensas Universitarias de la Universidad Autónoma de Madrid y la Universidad de Zaragoza, 1987), pp. 337–58; María Angeles Rodríguez Iglesias, *La mujer en la literatura: Una experiencia didáctica* (Pamplona, Gobierno de Navarra, Departamento de Bienestar Social, Deporte y Vivienda, Subdirección de la Mujer, 1993); Phyllis Zatlin, 'Women Novelists in Democratic Spain: Freedom to Express the Female Perspective', *Anales de la Literatura Española Contemporánea* 12 (1987), 29–44.

10. Elizabeth Ordóñez, 'Parody and Defiance: Subversive Challenges in the Texts of Díaz-Mas and Gómez Ojea', in *Voices of their Own: Contemporary Spanish Fiction by Women*, edited by E. Ordóñez (London, Associated Universities Press, 1991), pp. 149–73, and Zatlin, 'Women Novelists'.

11. The development of science fiction in Spain has been clearly traced by Carlos Saiz Cidoncha, *La ciencia ficción como fenómeno de comunicación y de cultura de masas* (Madrid, Editorial de la Universidad Complutense de Madrid, 1988) and Miguel Barceló, *Ciencia ficción: Guía de lectura* (Barcelona, Ediciones B Nova, Ciencia Ficción, 1990).

12. Dolores Robles Moreno, 'Escritoras españolas e hispanoamericanas de ciencia ficción' (Madrid, unpublished manuscript held at the Biblioteca de Mujeres, date unknown).

13. Darko Suvin, *Metamorphoses of Science Fiction: On the Poetics and History of a Literary Genre* (London, Yale University Press, 1979), p. 4.

14. Sarah Lefanu, *In the Chinks of the World Machine: Feminism and Science Fiction* (London, The Women's Press, 1988).

15. Jackson, Rosemary, *Fantasy: The Literature of Subversion* (London: Methuen, 1981), p. 8.

16. In Alejandro Gándara, 'Rosa Montero: "Somos esclavos de lo absurdo"', *El País*, 16 March 1988, 30.

17. Germán Gullón, 'El novelista como fabulador de la realidad: Mayoral, Guelbenzu, Merino …' in *Nuevos y novísimos: Algunas perspectivas críticas sobre la narrativa española desde la década de los sesenta* edited by Ricardo Landeira and Luis González del Valle (Boulder, Society of Spanish and Spanish American Studies, 1987), pp. 59–70 (p. 61).

18. Paloma Díaz-Mas, *El rapto del Santo Grial* (Barcelona, Anagrama, 1984), p. 10. Henceforth referred to as *RSG*.

19. In María Luz Diéguez, 'Entrevista con Paloma Díaz-Mas', *Revista de Estudios Hispánicos* 22:1 (1988), 84.

20. Juana Amelia Hernández, 'La postmodernidad en la ficción de Paloma Díaz-Mas', *Romance Languages Annual* 2 (1990), 450–4 (452).

21. Victoria Sendón de León et al., *Feminismo holístico: De la realidad a lo real* (Bilbao, Agora, 1994), pp. 93–115.

22. See Linda Gould Levine, 'The Female Body as Palimpsest in the Works of Carmen Gómez Ojea, Paloma Díaz-Mas and Ana Rossetti', *Indiana Journal of Hispanic Literatures* 2:1 (1993), 181–206 (194).

23. María Moliner, *Diccionario de uso del español* (Madrid, Gredos, 1990), p. 1381.

24. Rosa Montero, *Temblor* (Barcelona, Seix Barral, 1990). Henceforth referred to as *T.*

25. Phyllis Zatlin, 'The Novels of Rosa Montero as Experimental Fiction', *Monographic Review/Revista Monográfica* 8 (1992), 114–24; and 'Gothic Inversion of the Future: Rosa Montero's *Temblor*', *Romance Notes* 33:2 (1993), 119–23.

26. Catherine Davies, *Contemporary Feminist Fiction in Spain: The Work of Montserrat Roig and Rosa Montero* (Oxford, Berg, 1994), p. 151.

27. See José Manuel Fajardo 'Rosa Montero: "Los hombres inventan cuentos de hadas para explicarlo todo" ', *Cambio 16* 953 (1990), 100–3; and Rosa María Piñol 'Entrevista a Rosa Montero: "«Temblor» es mi primera novela cosmogónica" ', *La Vanguardia* 2 March 1990.

28. See Hernández, 'La postmodernidad'; Ordóñez 'Parody and Defiance'; Zatlin, 'The Novels of Rosa Montero'; Thomas R. Franz, 'Intertexts and Allusions as Aids to Meaning in Montero's *Temblor*', *Anales de la Literatura Española Contemporánea* 18 (1993), 261–79; and Kathleen Glenn, Review of *Temblor*, *Anales de la Literatura Española Contemporánea*, 16 (1991), 401–2.

29. Hart, Stephen, *White Ink: Essays on Twentieth Century Feminine Fiction in Spain and Latin America* (London, Tamésis, 1993), p. 133.

30. Biblioteca de Mujeres, 'Escritoras de ciencia ficción', *Madrid Feminista* 9 (1989), 4–5 (5).

31. Jochen Heymann and Montserrat Mullor-Heymann, *Retratos de escritorio: Entrevistas a autores españoles* (Frankfurt, Vervuert, 1991), p. 90.

32. Elia Barceló, *Consecuencia naturales* (Madrid, Miraguano, 1994). Henceforth referred to as *CN.*

33. Cristina Brullet Tenas, 'Roles e identidades de género: Una construcción social' in *Sociología de las mujeres españolas* edited by María Antonia García de León et al. (Madrid, Editorial Complutense, 1996), pp. 273–308.

34. Helen Graham and Jo Labanyi, 'Culture and Modernity: The Case of Spain' in *Spanish Cultural Studies: An Introduction* edited by Helen Graham and Jo Labanyi (Oxford, Oxford University Press, 1996), pp. 1–19 (pp. 17–18).

35. Jo Labanyi, 'Postmodernism and the Problem of Cultural Identity' in Graham and Labanyi (eds.), *Spanish Cultural Studies*, pp. 396–406 (pp. 403–4).

Gramsci and Spanish Cultural Studies

My aim here is to propose a variety of ways in which Gramsci's theories might be used to rethink the study of Spanish culture—and, if I am to be true to Gramsci's thought, I already need to indicate that by 'Spanish culture' I mean the many different cultures of the heterogeneous social groups comprising the geographical and political entity known as 'Spain'. Spanish academics have predominantly internalized French critical models, demonstrating a French cultural hegemony (Gramsci's term) that by the end of the 1970s had largely ceased to operate elsewhere, with the exception of the work of postmodern theorists such as Baudrillard and Lyotard—more influential in the United States than in France—and of cultural anthropologists such as Bourdieu—whose work on the manufacture of taste and on intellectuals has much in common with Gramsci's writings half a century before. It seems symptomatic that Spanish scholars should have identified themselves with Parisian rather than Southern European models, with the important exception of Spanish feminists who, in addition to French 'difference' feminism, have preferred Italian feminist theory to Anglo-Saxon varieties: a case, one suspects, of women whose aim is to theorize subalternity (again Gramsci's term) turning to models from a common Southern European heritage that itself occupies a subaltern position with regard to the global media pre-eminence of Anglo-Saxon culture. This general lack of knowledge of Italian cultural theory cuts Spanish scholars, and non-Spanish hispanists, off from insights into issues that have frequent relevance for Spain: that is, problems of uneven development and a north-south divide, a powerful Catholic Church co-existing with variegated forms of popular religion, the legacy of fascism, and the tensions between self-affirmation at national and local levels within a context of European integration and globalization. Although the European and global scenario is hugely changed since Gramsci's time, his appreciation that 'history is always "world history"'[1] and his understanding of hegemony and subalternity as cultural processes, seen crucially from the position of the subaltern, have much to offer on all these counts. Given the current emergence of trans-national political and economic configurations in the 'New Europe', it seems timely to encourage similar cultural rethinking across national boundaries. Not only is it absurd in the age of the global village for academic curricula to continue to be geared to the study of national cultures (a concept which corresponds to no one's experience of cultural consumption), but Spain and Italy have historically enjoyed considerable cultural interchange, not only with Aragón's past political control of southern Italy (including Gramsci's native Sardinia), but with the traffic of painters and musicians between the two countries from the Renaissance through the nineteenth century and, in the twentieth century, the close links between Italian and Spanish fascism and, conversely, the importance for the anti-Francoist cultural opposition of Italian neo-realism, which was explicitly based on Gramsci's concept of the national-popular (I shall return to this).

Before embarking on my list of research projects which might be facilitated through recourse to Gramsci's work, I need first to situate it within the development of cultural studies as a discipline—a history that many readers will be familiar with but which is not often considered in relation to hispanism. For the failure of Spanish and non-Spanish hispanists (with the important exception of Latin Americanists, as we shall see) to engage with Gramsci is synonymous with the failure, until very recently, to develop a cultural studies approach to the study of Spanish culture. Even though UK Departments of Spanish are starting to replace the traditional 'language and literature' diet with a broader menu of courses in 'language, literature and culture', this only makes explicit the assumption that language and literature will be studied in isolation from cultural processes. The basis of Gramsci's writings is his conviction that language and art cannot be studied in purely linguistic or artistic terms, for they have meaning only insofar as they express or mobilize cultural values—values which are always those of a particular social group or groups.

Fittingly for a discipline concerned with heterogeneity (a key legacy of Gramsci to cultural theory), cultural studies does not have a single origin. Its chief sources—all from the late 1920s–1930s and all developed in the context of political totalitarianism—are the work of the Frankfurt School (Benjamin, Adorno, Horkheimer); that of Gramsci, mostly during his eleven years of imprisonment under Mussolini as leader of the Italian Communist Party (1926–1937); and to a lesser extent that of Bakhtin in the Soviet Union, marginalized and later sentenced to inner exile under Stalin. Adorno and Horkheimer exported their broad political analysis of culture to the United States as refugees from Nazism; their suspicion of mass culture, which as a result of their experience of Nazi cultural manipulation they saw as a strategy for reducing the populace to passive acquiescence, took root among 1940s and 50s US intellectuals worried about the negative effects of late capitalist consumer culture. As is well known, this worry also underlay the work of Raymond Williams and the early Birmingham Centre for Contemporary Cultural Studies, under Richard Hoggart, in the 1950s. But Williams' and Hoggart's redemptive concern with the communal values of the working-class environments from which both came led them also to look to Gramsci, who, unlike Adorno and Horkheimer, appreciated the strengths of popular culture and its capacity for survival and resistance. The fact that Gramsci came from underdeveloped Sardinia, just as Williams and Hoggart came from working-class backgrounds, is crucial here. Most fundamentally, Williams and Hoggart took from Gramsci a refusal to see the subaltern as passive objects of cultural manipulation from above, and a converse insistence on seeing them as thinking subjects endowed, within the limits of their historical circumstances, with agency. As Gramsci put it, everyone is an intellectual but only some have the social advantages and cultural training that make it possible to turn 'common sense' (whose positive as well as negative features Gramsci appreciated) into 'good sense'.

As Brandist notes,[2] the work of Bakhtin, 'discovered' in the West in the late 1970s as an antidote to the formalist excesses of French structuralism, parallels that of Gramsci in its concern with cultural heterogeneity. Bakhtin's starting point was his repudiation of the ahistoricist universalism of Saussure's linguistic theories. The appropriation of Gramsci and Bakhtin by British cultural studies coincided with a revaluation of the work of Walter Benjamin who, while sharing many of Adorno and Horkheimer's misgivings about capitalist cultural commodification, nevertheless was sensitive to the cultural possibilities opened up by capitalist modernity, and particularly to the possibilities afforded the cultural historian by the fragmentation of modern life, permitting new ways of thinking through a process of cultural scavenging and montage. What Gramsci, Bakhtin and Benjamin have in common is a belief in individual agency, and a stress on cultural heterogeneity, ambivalence and contradiction that undermines all political attempts at enforcing homogeneity. As is well known, this has made their thought invaluable to left-wing thinkers wanting to construct alternative cultural models to orthodox Marxism, firstly during the Cold War, and subsequently through the process of de-stalinization and eventual collapse of communism. Especially important here is the stress by all three thinkers on culture as the means by which power relations are brokered, for various reasons. Firstly, this gives a role to intellectuals. Secondly and crucially, their well known refusal to see economics as the sole or prime determining factor allows a space for agency, for, while economic systems are normally imposed on the majority, cultural identities are the result of a two-way interchange, in which the subaltern can, through a process of mimicry (a concept developed by Gramsci long before contemporary cultural theory), appropriate aspects of dominant culture for their own strategic purposes.

Gramsci's stress on the recycling and mimicry fundamental to popular culture, dovetailing in many respects with Bakhtin's work on the carnivalesque, has made both thinkers crucial to the development of post-colonial studies, from Fanon through to Bhabha, and to the multiculturalism central to contemporary postmodern theory. Indeed, Gramsci's and Bakhtin's insistence on seeing culture as a site of struggle between a plurality of dominant and subaltern constituencies, each of which is in turn a mixture of heterogeneous tendencies vying for dominance, provides an important political reminder that postmodern free play is never free and never just a game. If Gramsci's and Bakhtin's political analysis of cultural heterogeneity has made them central to current attempts to theorize multiculturalism in the United States, Britain and also Australia, here Gramsci's work has an advantage over that of Bakhtin. For, while both analyse the possibilities of popular contestation to dominant discourses afforded by cultural heterogeneity, Bakhtin chiefly situates such contestatory spaces in the pre-modern world, whereas Gramsci is equally appreciative of the heterogeneous mix of reactionary and progressive tendencies in peasant culture (which he never archaizes as a primitive throwback) and in modern mass culture. In this sense, Gramsci's work can usefully complement Benjamin's analysis of the contradictory fissures within bourgeois modernity which open up spaces of resistance.

It is no coincidence that Gramsci and Benjamin should have been seminal influences on Latin American cultural theory, for their conjunction provides a formidable framework for theorizing the complexities of uneven development: that is, the coexistence of the pre-modern, the modern and the postmodern—or perhaps one should say, the coexistence of the pre-modern and the modern which is itself a key feature of postmodernity. Here Gramsci's notion of culture as a negotiation process between a multiplicity of internally heterogeneous dominant and subaltern groups has productively joined forces with the Cuban anthropologist Fernando Ortiz's rejection—in his seminal work *Contrapunteo cubano del tabaco y el azúcar* (1940)[3]—of the concept of acculturation, according to which the subaltern passively assimilate cultural forms imposed from above, for the notion of transculturation, whereby the subaltern selectively appropriate and resemanticize for their own purposes those elements of the dominant culture that are useful to them. Ortiz was, of course, developing his cultural theories in the 20s and 30s, coinciding with Gramsci, and again largely under dictatorial regimes. The reworking of Ortiz's theories by Angel Rama in the 70s[4] parallels the contemporaneous reworking of Gramsci's thought in Britain. Indeed, Néstor García Canclini, in his influential book *Culturas híbridas: estrategias para entrar y salir de la modernidad*,[5] brings together the insights of Ortiz as read by Rama and of Gramsci as read by Raymond Williams.

Why, then, has the work of Gramsci—so productive for Latin American cultural theory, particularly with the recent development in the US of subaltern studies—not been used in the study of Spanish culture? There are, I think, multiple reasons, and I shall discuss only some of them here. First is the lamentable fact that the only major cultural theorist produced by twentieth-century Spain—at least, prior to the work of the US-based contemporary urban theorist Manuel Castells—has been Ortega y Gasset, whose perceptive insights into the avant-garde were predicated on a typically modernist desire to distance high cultural experimentation from the rapidly growing mass culture industries. That is, commercial publishing developments such as the popular novella sold by weekly subscription (exploited by, among others, the feminist Carmen de Burgos and the anarchist Salvador Seguí); the radio, disseminating an already flourishing music hall repertoire blending popular and mass cultural forms;[6] and above all the cinema, fusing modernist spatial and temporal dislocation with premodern folklore and nineteenth-century mass cultural forms such as melodrama. While Ortega's theories of 'dehumanization' may be partially useful, they totally fail to appreciate the cultural hybridity that characterizes the Spanish avant-garde perhaps more than any other: I shall come back to this when proposing an alternative Gramscian reading. In failing to acknowledge the validity and vitality of popular and mass culture, Ortega was by implication reinforcing the privileging of the Northern European over the Southern European that characterizes his work from his first book *Meditaciones del Quijote* (1914) on; that is, the notion that Latin cultures are congenitally inferior in their attention to the concrete, by comparison with the capacity for intellectual abstraction evidenced in Germanic cultures.[7] The cultural capital involved in Ortega's dissociation of himself from his Latin cultural environment is obvious (it should be noted here that, although 'cultural capital' is Bourdieu's term, the concept is central to Gramsci's work). The lionizing of Ortega by centre-right disaffected Francoist intellectuals, and above all by centre-left Republican exiles who trained a whole generation of United States hispanists (many of whom have been aggressively hostile to the introduction of cultural studies into the curriculum), has helped perpetuate the notion that Spanish culture is inferior—a notion that hispanists, competing in a world of diminishing academic resources with their colleagues in larger English and French Departments, have been all too ready to internalize.

My central argument here is that a re-reading of Spanish culture in terms of Gramsci's valorization of popular and mass culture (albeit recognizing their mix of reactionary and progressive elements) allows us to propose Spain, not as an implicitly inferior exception to Europe's rule, but as a paradigmatic case of the importance of popular and mass culture in negotiating viable forms of cultural identity—something that is true of all nations, but which those that underwent capitalist modernization earliest and most thoroughly have been able to 'forget' in their desire to present bourgeois cultural forms as universal. Adrian Shubert, in his excellent *A Social History of Modern Spain*,[8] has similarly argued that Spain should not be seen as an exception and failure in relation to a supposed European 'norm' because its 'bourgeois revolution' took place at a time when the bourgeoisie was a minority, for that was true for the majority of European nations, including France and Germany. Shubert is currently writing a book on bullfighting demonstrating that this popular cultural form, traditionally seen as a mark of Spain's barbaric if picturesque backwardness, is better read as an early instance of capitalist commodification of the leisure industries. Timothy Mitchell, in his wonderful book *Flamenco Deep Song*,[9] has done something similar with flamenco, arguing that it should be seen, not as a primitive relic of pure racial (gypsy) origins, but as the hybrid product of urban modernity, developing as an art form in the second half of the nineteenth century as migration to the cities brought together a new urban lumpenproletariat (called *gitanos* but an 'ethnic chaos' of marginal elements) and the *señoritos* (landowners' sons) who paid them to perform. In Mitchell's acute formulation, flamenco was the product of an 'urban drinking subculture', inextricably mixed with prostitution, based on the underclasses' collusion with their paymasters in a way that allowed them to turn collusion to their advantage as a strategy for survival if not social advancement. Mitchell's debt to Gramsci here is indirect but substantial. One of Gramsci's major insights, appropriated by post-colonial theorists, is the ability of the subaltern to turn their position of weakness to their advantage, not through direct class confrontation (where they would lose), but by using collusion to exert a degree of control over their superiors, in what Gramsci would call a 'counter-hegemonic' tactic. By studying popular cultural practices, both Shubert and Mitchell have been able to show that cultural forms that have been taken as a sign of Spain's 'difference' from developed northern Europe—bullfighting and flamenco—are in fact classic examples of the hybridization of popular and mass cultural forms that typifies capitalist modernity but which the dominant bourgeois classes have marginalized, either by dismissing such cultural manifestations as 'low culture', or by endowing them with a spurious myth of primitive origins.

The richness and diversity of Spain's popular cultural forms were of course stressed by Francoism, which at the same time relegated them to an inferior 'feminine' status by entrusting their preservation to the Women's Section of the Spanish Fascist Party, Sección Femenina. This, following on Ortega's privileging of elite cultural forms (against which it was a typically fascist philistine reaction), has no doubt clinched negative academic perceptions of Spanish popular culture as retrograde and anti-modern: that is, a fascist fantasy of organic rural wholeness (as in early Francoist ideology), or a tourist's dream of romantic, orientalist 'otherness' (as in Fraga Iribarne's notorious tourist slogan of the 60s, 'Spain is different', which typified later Francoist attitudes to popular culture). But both of these definitions alert us to the fact that such nostalgic views of popular culture are themselves signs of cultural hybridity: in this case, of a conservative modernity's attempt to obtain hegemony by idealizing supposedly premodern cultural forms through capitalist techniques of cultural commodification—the cinema, as famously in the folkloric film musical of the 1940s and early 50s (about which more later), and from the late 1950s the international tourist industry. As Shubert's and Mitchell's studies show, this cultural hybridity, typically regarded as the mark of postmodernism, can be traced back to the beginnings of the modernization process, with the dominant classes' co-option of popular and mass cultural forms, the amalgamation of popular cultural traditions with modern mass culture through rural migration to the cities, and the consequent subaltern collusion with dominant culture. Indeed, the continuum between traditional popular and modern mass culture created by continuing migration to the cities throughout the twentieth century, and more recently by the passage of sectors of the population directly from pre-modern oral culture to the secondary orality of the postmodern media, has produced a particularly interesting case of cultural heterogeneity, in which the progressive and the retrograde mingle and can be mobilized—whether by the mass media or by audiences—for contrary ends. One of the advantages of Gramsci's term 'subaltern' is that it covers both the rural and urban lower classes, departing from classic Marxist theory by seeing them as a continuum. The particularly strong interrelation in Spain between popular and mass culture again allows the Spanish case to stand as a reminder of a cultural interdependence often underestimated or forgotten in studies of northern Europe or the United States (where mass European immigration came predominantly from peasant stock, much of it from southern Italy).

So far I have argued that, if the concentration on high cultural forms betrays an anxious desire on the part of hispanists (Spanish and otherwise) to prove that Spanish culture is not inferior, conversely study of Spain's particularly interesting and complex mix of popular and mass cultural forms allows Spain to emerge, not as the exception to Europe's rule, but as a paradigmatic model of the importance of culture, and particularly of the complex transactions between high, popular and mass cultural forms, in the nation-formation process. I should like now to take some moments in that nation-formation process, starting with the late nineteenth-century Restoration period, and to ask—briefly—how Gramsci's theories might be used to read these historical junctures in cultural terms.

Gramsci is primarily known for his often misunderstood concept of the 'national-popular',[10] by which he meant the need for the Italian Communist Party to obtain hegemony by winning the broad-based cultural allegiance of the masses, by contrast with previous bourgeois nation-formation projects which had been based on the cultural exclusion of the mass of the populace, apart from the co-option of select individuals (what Gramsci dismissed as 'volunteerism'—Ortega's notion of a meritocracy based on rule by a select minority is, one may note, a perfect example). Much of Gramsci's work was devoted to analysing the failings of the bourgeois nation-formation process that took place on Italy's unification in 1861—a process that, historical differences apart, paralleled the intense concern with nation formation under the Restoration in Spain by both Cánovas's Conservatives and Sagasta's Liberals (an intensification of the liberal centralizing project that had begun in the mid century with the disentailment acts, the construction of a radial railway network, and the removal of internal tariffs creating a national market). Gramsci's analysis of this mid-to-late nineteenth-century nation-formation process has direct relevance for an understanding of the Spanish realist novel, and especially that of Galdós, as I hope briefly to indicate. One of Gramsci's chief concerns was with the fact that the Italian mass reading public, in the nineteenth century and still in his day, almost exclusively read foreign authors. Gramsci consistently dismissed the bourgeois belief that art should be judged solely by the aesthetic criterion of beauty as an elitist tactic for excluding the popular, arguing that artistic products (bourgeois and otherwise) needed always to be 'read' in cultural terms; that is, by looking at how they did or did not engage with the mindset and lifestyles of their audiences (with what Raymond Williams, basing himself on Gramsci, would later call 'a structure of feeling'). Popular taste is thus seen by Gramsci as an index of the masses' cultural concerns in the broadest sense. He consequently concluded that the way for the Italian Communist Party to shape popular opinion and thus secure political hegemony was through popular culture—not in the sense of imposing values on the people from above, but in that of enabling the people to give coherent expression to what mattered to them. If the nineteenth-century Italian popular reading public read foreign, primarily French, writers, that—Gramsci observed—indicated that foreign popular writers articulated matters of concern to them in a way that Italian writers had failed to do. Gramsci thus argued for the need for Italian writers to draw on popular fiction 'with its tastes and tendencies and its moral and intellectual world, even if it is backward and conventional' (Forgacs and Nowell-Smith, 102), in the way that Dostoyevsky had done in Russia, in order to create a national-popular literature that would enable the masses to articulate their at present incoherently formulated needs and desires.

The Restoration period in Spain saw a concerted drive to create a national novel, in response to the perceived flood of imported popular fiction; Galdós's 1870 essay 'Observaciones sobre la novela contemporánea en España',[11] written as he was about to embark on his novelistic career, makes just this point. It would be useful to investigate the extent to which this process of canon formation corresponded to a bourgeois exclusionary project, and to what extent it catered to a more democratic concern to give expression to the national masses. A central debate of the period was that between Cánovas's Doctrinaire Liberal centralizing project, and the defence of local and individual freedoms by Sagasta's Progressive Liberals (for which Galdós became a Deputy in 1886) and by the Republicans (supported throughout his life by the other major novelist of the period, Leopoldo Alas). (I leave

Emilia Pardo Bazán out here since, despite her radical stance on gender, her position on class was clearly exclusionary.) Galdós's own novelistic project seems to me to obey Gramsci's prescriptions for a national-popular literature to a remarkable degree. For a start, such a reading helps explain why, despite his dismissal of cheap imported melodramas, he incorporated the structures of melodrama into his own work (a contradiction that Stephanie Sieburth has shown also to characterize Alas's *La Regenta*[12]). More centrally, Galdós's much praised concern with the varieties and nuances of popular speech can be seen as an attempt to give voice to the heterogeneous social constituencies comprising the nation. Craig Brandist (1996) observes that the main parallel between Gramsci's thought and that of Bakhtin is the concern of both with linguistic diversity; indeed, as David Forgacs notes (Forgacs and Nowell-Smith, 164–7), Gramsci's political concept of hegemony was based on the theories of linguistic diffusion elaborated by the school of 'neo-linguistics' or 'spatial linguistics' at Turin University where Gramsci studied for his unfinished doctoral thesis in historical linguistics.

I would thus propose that the evident Bakhtinian heteroglossia or dialogism of Galdós's novels (another instance of Cervantine influence) be read in terms of an attempt to create a national-popular novel that acknowledges rather than erases cultural difference. Galdós's journalistic as well as fictional writings constantly lament the increasing standardization of modern life; his *Novelas contemporáneas*, which insist on preserving linguistic variety, treat sympathetically their lower-class characters' resistance to the various agents of social control who try to 'normalize' their behaviour.[13] The failed schoolmaster and even worse popular novelist, José Ido, who corrects spelling mistakes in the street, is depicted as a madman; Galdós's notoriously unreliable narrators similarly signify refusal of an authoritarian monologic vision.[14] Particularly significant here is Galdós's decision in his major novel *Fortunata y Jacinta* (1886–7), defying all classical rules of artistic unity, to switch from the bourgeois focalizers of Part 1 and to focalize Parts 2–4 predominantly through his uneducated working-class heroine. While all of Galdós's fiction bears testimony to the linguistic mimicry by which the various lower social strata negotiate a *modus vivendi* with their superiors, *Fortunata y Jacinta* also shows the reverse process by which the bourgeois Juanito mimics the linguistic idiosyncrasies of the urban underclasses, which for him constitute a kind of primitive 'nature reserve' (the word he famously uses is 'cantera' or quarry). Here Juanito exemplifies what Gramsci would dismiss as a typically bourgeois archaizing concept of folklore, which fails to appreciate it—as Galdós's novel evidently does—as the living expression of a world view, internally heterogeneous and contradictory, incorporating reactionary and progressive tendencies. For Gramsci, as for Galdós, folklore is not confined to the peasantry but is the expression of subaltern 'common sense'; that is, a 'structure of feeling' (to use Williams's later formulation) that is entirely valid but needing to be given coherent, conscious articulation. I think it would be hard to find a better expression of Galdós's vast fictional project for mapping the nation: one which stands as a counter-project to the centralizing legislation of successive Cánovas governments, whose concern with social standardization—that is, the imposition of a monolithic concept of the nation—was logically enough accompanied by the repeated restriction of suffrage.

The principal champions of local and individual freedoms under the Restoration were the Krausists, whose successors—through their secular educational establishment, the Institución Libre de Enseñanza, and its university offshoot, the Residencia de Estudiantes—provided a base for the particularly brilliant avant-garde that developed in Spain in the later 1920s, as well as training the majority of government ministers of the Second Republic in the 1930s. The only study I know that gives the Krausists the respect they deserve as major political thinkers is that by Elías Díaz, sadly long out of print.[15] They are best known outside Spain through López-Morillas's studies,[16] which construct them as idealist, puritanical cranks: a view that the most cursory reading of their political writings shows to be entirely untenable. One of the Krausists' favourite concepts is that of the need for an organic society, by which they meant a plural society in which the various individual 'organs' respected and worked actively to support the others (hence their rejection of French centralist political models, as of Hegel's Statism, turning instead to the work of J.S. Mill). One of Gramsci's key concepts is, of course, that of the 'organic' intellectual, who respects cultural pluralism by trying to view the way of life ('folklore') of the various subaltern groups from the inside, in order to help such groups, through education and popular culture, articulate their aspirations. Only in this way, according to Gramsci, could the Italian Communist Party achieve hegemony (that is, consent obtained through cultural allegiance) as opposed to domination. There is, I think, an urgent need to attempt a study of the Krausists and their 1920s and 30s *institucionista* offspring in the light of Gramsci's concept of the 'organic' intellectual. Whether they would entirely fit Gramsci's blueprint is unclear, for despite their championship of cultural pluralism their notion of 'social improvement' was largely a top-down one based on bourgeois concepts of individual autonomy and propriety (including property). But at the same time the studies of folklore undertaken by the father of the later Republican poet Antonio Machado, and Giner de los Ríos's famous promotion of geographic excursions to acquaint his largely bourgeois pupils (including Antonio Machado) with the rural hinterland can be read in terms of a Gramscian project for procuring an alliance between intellectuals and the people based on the former's attempts to understand the culture of the latter. That such understanding was the other side of a giant Foucauldian surveillance project is undeniably true, as evidenced most explicitly by the 1883–9 Comisión de Reformas Sociales [Social Reform Commission], initiated by the Krausist minister Segismundo Moret in order to document every aspect of lower-class life. The Krausists' promotion of geographic excursions also included participation in expeditions to Central Africa paving the way for colonial expansion, seen by them as an 'extension of civilization and promotion of culture'.[17] And, despite my previous point about Galdós's and Alas's recourse to melodrama, the cultural tastes of the Krausists on the whole remained within the confines of bourgeois aestheticism, though I suspect that a re-reading of Giner de los Ríos's writings on art in the light of Gramsci's theories of the national-popular might produce a significantly different, and more positive, valuation.[18]

I would also propose such a reading of the relationship between the avant-garde artists of the 1927 Generation and the *institucionista*-based Residencia de Estudiantes, which has largely been seen as a privileged cosmopolitan space exposing young writers and artists, through its programme of visiting lectures, to current European intellectual and artistic trends. Much of the theoretical work on the European avant-garde, predicated on an Orteguian rejection of mass and popular culture, fails to do justice to the particularly fertile interrelationship in the work of the Spanish avant-garde between high cultural experiment and both folk culture and modern mass culture. The appropriation of folk culture in the music of Falla and the poetry and drama of Lorca is well known; Catherine Davies has suggested that Lorca's appeal to peasant culture in his plays of the 1930s may have been influenced by his encounter in Cuba with Fernando Ortiz, who was responsible for inviting him to the island in 1930.[19] The most obvious examples of the assimilation of modern mass culture are the use of cinematic motifs and structures in Alberti's poetry and Gómez de la Serna's experimental prose, not to mention Valle-Inclán's fiction and drama of the 1920s, Lorca's surrealist writing (including the film script *Viaje a la luna* [Trip to the Moon]), and of course Buñuel and Dalí's early cinematic partnership.[20]

But one should also remember the cult of the fairground in Maruja Mallo's *Verbena* paintings of 1928 and Giménez Caballero's film *Esencia de verbena* of 1930. What Mallo's paintings of Madrid fairgrounds show so well is the continuum between popular (rural) and mass (urban) culture which led Gramsci to reject Marx's negative valorization of the peasantry. Néstor García Canclini's *Culturas híbridas*, mentioned above, argues that the most brilliant avant-gardes have occurred, not in developed northern Europe or the United States, but in countries— whether Latin or Latin American—characterized by uneven development, where the contrast between new and old ways of life created a particularly strong sense of cultural dislocation. It is logical that the dislocations and dissonances found in the work of the Spanish avant-garde should so often be expressed through the seemingly incongruous juxtaposition of popular (traditional) and mass (modern) cultural forms.

What is not clear, to me at least, is the extent to which their incorporation of popular cultural forms responds to an elitist and ultimately bourgeois primitivist project, and the extent to which it might be seen as the expression of a Gramscian attempt to construct a national-popular culture, whereby the artist as 'organic intellectual' embraces subaltern cultural forms while respecting their diversity. This said, I would propose that a reading of the surrealist love of incongruity, and consistent refusal to assimilate diversity into a unitary vision, might benefit from a political reading in terms of Gramsci's insistence on the need for a national-popular culture that respects heterogeneity. Although surrealist dissonance was not always based on the incongruous juxtaposition of different class elements, I suspect that thinking about it in such Gramscian terms might produce more examples than expected —in the case of the Spanish avant-garde at least. Gramsci's own relationship with the Italian futurists was, as is well known, a fraught one: having invited Marinetti to mount an art exhibition at the Institute of Proletarian Culture in Turin which he helped set up, after the futurists' defection to fascism he dismissed them as 'A group of schoolboys who escaped from a Jesuit boarding school, whooped it up in a nearby wood and were led back under the policeman's stick' (Forgacs and Nowell-Smith, 18–19). The strength of reference in the work of the Spanish avant-garde to popular as well as modern mass culture lends itself to a Gramscian reading even better than the work of the Italian futurists, though in Spain as elsewhere avant-garde experiment appealed to radicals of the right as well as the left. It seems significant that the writer who exclusively championed modern mass culture, Giménez

Caballero, should have swung to the right, while those who also paid attention to popular culture tended to support centre-left or left positions under the Second Republic. It must, however, be noted that 1930s attempts by intellectuals and students to take culture to the rural populace—the Republican Government-financed Misiones Pedagógicas and Lorca's travelling theatre company La Barraca—were seemingly not interested in undertaking a Gramscian ethnographic enquiry into popular life, but rather in disseminating knowledge of the national classics to the illiterate; the Golden Age plays which they staged for peasant audiences had, of course, originally played to a broad social public prior to bourgeois modernity's reinforcement of the 'high'/'low' cultural divide. In proposing Gramsci's concepts of the 'organic intellectual' and of the national-popular as frameworks for studying the Krausist-formed institucionistas and the 1920s avant-garde who were so closely linked to them, I am not suggesting that they be neatly fitted into a new label but rather that Gramsci's contemporaneous reading of the relationship between intellectuals and culture may help us appreciate the often contradictory political implications of their cultural practice.

In his book on flamenco, Timothy Mitchell is scathing about Falla's and Lorca's famous Granada flamenco competition of 1922, which he sees as a primitivist co-option of popular culture for high cultural purposes, supposedly 'rescuing' it from 'contamination' at the hands of modern mass culture and restoring it to a spurious 'primitive purity' (in practice, fossilizing it). As Mitchell notes, at the time flamenco was thriving in various hybrid forms in modern mass culture (i.e. the music hall) and did not need rescuing by bourgeois intellectuals—a salvage attempt that would be repeated with the flamenco revival by Francoist intellectuals in the 1950s. This raises the problem of distinguishing between Gramsci's notion of the national-popular and populism. Gramsci himself was clear about the difference although he too would be accused of populism by the 1960s Italian New Left (Forgacs and Nowell-Smith, 196). For Gramsci, the crucial difference was that populism, as seen clearly in its fascist variety, promoted an idealized vision of popular culture in order to secure mass adherence to a monolithic model of the nation; whereas the national-popular signified the attempt by intellectuals to understand and represent the world view of subaltern groups. One of Gramsci's strengths is his acknowledgement and understanding of the appeal of fascism to certain subaltern groups since, contrary to bourgeois capitalist cultural elitism, it mobilized popular culture—largely through the mass-cultural media—albeit for anti-democratic ends. Gramsci wrote appreciatively of Mussolini's early socialist phase, and indeed in some ways his concept of the national-popular was developed in prison in order to assimilate for the left the lessons learnt from the valorization of popular culture that had enabled fascism to win popular support.

I have discussed elsewhere the usefulness of Gramsci's writings on folklore for an understanding of the folkloric film musical or *folklórica* which was used by both the Republic and early Francoism as a tool of very different nation-formation projects, which can be called national-popular and populist respectively.[21] Here I will limit myself to noting that Gramsci's understanding of the appeal of fascist populism helps explain the awkward fact that the early Francoist *folklórica* was massively popular, especially with the lower classes and women—the two constituencies who most suffered under Francoism. Gramsci's analysis of the complex bargaining processes that constitute hegemony also enables us to appreciate that the early Francoist *folklórica* gives a much less monolithic account of cultural formations that is normally supposed. Indeed, the genre's stock romance plots consist in the usually gypsy trickster heroine securing marriage to the usually land-owning male protagonist through a series of negotiations (often dramatized through battles between classical, mass and popular musical forms) that force him to capitulate to her popular cultural values. Performance style and camerawork ensure that audience identifications are entirely on the side of the subaltern trickster heroine, through whom the narrative is always focalized. As I have argued elsewhere, these films offer considerable scope for counter-hegemonic readings by subaltern groups; indeed they force all spectators to occupy the vantage-point of the subaltern, trickster, usually 'other-race' heroine—at least until the conventional romance ending assimilates difference into a fantasy of social harmony. It must be remembered that early Francoism was also fond of the term 'organic'. Although its Francoist usage was totally different from that of Gramsci, or that of the Krausists and their Republican heirs, in all three cases its use points to a positive valorization of folklore in the broad Gramscian sense of the world view of the subaltern, in all three cases seen as dynamic and capable of adapting to modernity—whether conceived in progressive or conservative terms. Ethnographic research in Spain could benefit from Gramsci's entirely non-primitivist political reading of folklore's contradictory reactionary and progressive potential, which allows such political slippage but also ensures that some progressive potential remains in even its most retrograde appropriations.

I shall close by proposing two more research projects which would be facilitated by a reading of Gramsci's work. Both are obvious but to my knowledge have not been attempted. The first is an analysis of the Gramscian basis (or departures from it) of the oppositional culture which emerged in Spain in the 1950s, first with Spanish neo-realist cinema and, from 1954, with the social realist novel. Spanish neo-realist cinema consciously modelled itself on Italian neo-realism, itself an conscious implementation of Gramsci's notion of the national-popular. As David Forgacs notes (Forgacs and Nowell-Smith, 196), in 1950s Italy the terms 'national popular' and 'neo-realism', together with that of 'social realism', became virtually synonymous. Given the slippage observed above between fascist populism and the national-popular, it is not surprising that Spanish neo-realist cinema should have been inaugurated by the disaffected Falangist director Nieves Conde, with his 1951 film *Surcos*. In practice, much Spanish neo-realist cinema and social realist fiction, like its Italian counterparts, evolved into satirical debunkings of the pro-regime elite—the class from which most 1950s Spanish opposition intellectuals came. The public for Spanish neo-realist cinema and social realist fiction remained confined to a university-educated minority. Indeed, it was only in the course of the 1980s that the Spanish mass reading public, perhaps for the first time in its history, came to prefer Spanish writers to foreign ones.[22] Here the contrast with contemporary cinema audiences is marked, with Spanish films rarely breaking into the mass market.[23]

This brings me to my final research proposal: that is, an ethnographic analysis of audience reception in one or more specific periods of recent Spanish history, based on systematic fieldwork aimed at ascertaining the correlation between those cultural products on the market and the 'structure of feeling' of those groups who consumed them. Although Gramsci could not have anticipated the power of today's globalized marketing and distribution networks, his hypothesis that, if the mass public prefers foreign works it is because these correspond more closely to their cultural needs and desires than domestic output, seems likely to be productive—particularly in analysis of the mass public for imported films and fiction. I hope myself to contribute to such research through a collaborative 'Oral History of Cinema-Going in 1940s and 1950s Spain', planned with Vicente Sánchez Biosca in Spain, and Kathleen Vernon and Susan Martín-Márquez in the US. It would not have been possible to formulate such a project without an acquaintance with Gramsci's political understanding of culture as a negotiation process between competing social groups, which does not just reflect their position with regard to power but enables them, within the limits of the historically possible, to modify it. I shall conclude by citing Gramsci's unorthodox Marxist formulation of the instrumental, rather than representational, function of culture, in this case in the form of language, viewed in terms of the modern mass cultural metaphor of photography:

Grammar is [...] the 'photograph' of a given phase of a national (collective) language that has been formed historically and is continuously developing [...]. The practical question might be: what is the purpose of such a photograph? To record the history of an aspect of civilization or to modify an aspect of civilization? (Forgacs and Nowell-Smith, 179–80).

JO LABANYI
Birkbeck College, University of London

NOTES

1. Antonio Gramsci, *Selections from Cultural Writings*, edited by David Forgacs and Geoffrey Nowell-Smith (Cambridge, Mass., Harvard University Press, 1985), p. 181. My discussion of Gramsci's work is largely based on the texts in this anthology and on Marcia Landy's *Film, Politics, and Gramsci* (Minneapolis and London, University of Minnesota Press, 1994).
2. Craig Brandist, 'Gramsci, Bakhtin and the Semiotics of Hegemony', *New Left Review* 216 (1996), 94–109.
3. Translated into English by Harriet de Onís as *Cuban Counterpoint: Tobacco and Sugar* (Durham, N.C., Duke University Press, 1995).
4. Angel Rama, 'Processes of Transculturation in Latin American Narrative' reproduced in *Journal of Latin American Cultural Studies* 6:2 (1997), 155–71. Originally published in *Revista de Literatura Iberoamericana* 5 (April 1974). See also his elaboration of the concept in *Transculturación narrativa en América Latina* (Mexico City, Siglo XXI, 1982).
5. Nestor García Canclini, *Culturas híbridas: estrategias para entrar y salir de la modernidad* (Mexico City, Grijalbo, 1990); English translation *Hybrid Cultures* (Minneapolis, University of Minnesota Press, 1995).
6. For the popular novella and radio transmission of popular song, see respectively José Alvarez Junco, 'Rural and Urban Popular Cultures' and Serge Salaün, 'The *Cuplé*: Modernity and Mass Culture', both in *Spanish Cultural Studies: An Introduction*, edited by Helen Graham and Jo Labanyi (Oxford, Oxford University Press, 1995), pp. 82–90 and pp. 90–4.
7. This criticism of Ortega's cultural elitism was made a long time ago by John Butt in his *Writers and Politics in Modern Spain* (London, Hodder and Stoughton, 1978), which can usefully be re-read in the context of the revalorization of popular and mass culture by contemporary cultural studies.

8. Adrian Shubert, *A Social History of Modern Spain* (London, Unwin Hyman, 1990); see the introduction 'Spain and Europe: the Peculiarities of the Historians', pp. 1–6.

9. Timothy Mitchell, *Flamenco Deep Song* (New Haven and London, Yale University Press, 1994).

10. See David Forgacs, 'National-popular: genealogy of a concept', in *The Cultural Studies Reader*, edited by Simon During (London and New York, Routledge, 1993), pp. 177–90.

11. Reprinted in Galdós, *Ensayos de crítica literaria*, edited by Laureano Bonet (Barcelona, Península, 1972), pp. 115–32; and in English in *Galdós*, edited by Jo Labanyi (London, Longman, 1993), pp. 29–34.

12. Stephanie Sieburth, *Reading 'La Regenta': Duplicitous Discourse and the Entropy of Structure* (Amsterdam and Philadelphia, John Benjamins, 1990).

13. See Teresa Fuentes Peris, 'Visions of Filth: Deviancy and Social Control in the Novels of Galdós' (PhD thesis, University of London, 1997); and my own forthcoming *Gender and Modernization in the Spanish Realist Novel* (Oxford University Press).

14. Galdós's recourse—most notably in *El amigo Manso* (1882), *La de Bringas* (1884), *Lo prohibido* (1884–5), *Fortunata y Jacinta* (1886–7) and *Nazarín* (1895)—to unreliable character-narrators has commonly been seen as a mark of Cervantine self-reflexivity, ironically undermining the realism which the text at the same time creates. What needs stressing is that this ambivalent realist project which undermines its own premises is, in Galdós's case, a critique of the nation-formation process of which the realist novel was a major instrument.

15. Elías Díaz, *La filosofía social del krausismo español* (Madrid, Edicusa, 1973).

16. Juan López-Morillas, *The Krausist Movement and Ideological Change in Spain, 1854–1874* (Cambridge, Cambridge University Press, 1981) (Spanish original *El krausismo español: perfil de una aventura intelectual*, 1936); *Krausismo: estética y literatura*, 2nd edn (Barcelona, Lumen, 1990).

17. The terms used in an 1884 letter from the Institución Libre's Rector, expressing 'unreserved support' for the activities of the Sociedad de Africanistas y Colonistas; quoted in José Antonio Rodríguez Esteban, 'La Institución Libre de Enseñanza y la Sociedad Geográfica de Madrid. La Geografía decimonónica en la regeneración interior e exterior de España', *Boletín de la Institución Libre de Enseñanza*, II Época, 19 (April 1994), 33–44 (40). Rodríguez Esteban demonstrates the Institución Libre's links with the Sociedad Española para la Exploración y Civilización del Africa Central (1877–1883) and its successor, the Sociedad de Africanistas y Colonistas, founded after the Congreso de Geografía Colonial y Mercantil of 1883.

18. For Giner de los Ríos's writings on art see his *Estudios literarios* (Madrid, 1866), and vol. 3, *Estudios de literatura y arte* (1919) of his *Obras completas* (Madrid, 1916–36); also López-Morillas, *Krausismo*.

19. Catherine Davies, '*María Antonia*: tragedia cubana, tanto africana como hispana', in *Actas del Primer Congreso Anglo-Hispano*, edited by Alan

Deyermond and Ralph Penny, vol. 2, *Literatura* (Madrid, Castalia, 1993), pp. 287–97 (291–5.) Davies has further explored the significance of Ortiz's work in 'The transculturation process: Fernando Ortiz's version', unpublished paper given at the conference *1498–1998: Raízes, Rotas, Reflexoes*, Braga (Portugal), 6–11 September 1998.

20. The influence of the cinema on the Spanish avant-garde has been studied by C.B. Morris in *This Loving Darkness: The Cinema and Spanish Writers 1920–1936* (Oxford, Oxford University Press and University of Hull, 1980).

21. Papers at the Institute of Romance Studies, June 1997, and at the Crossroads Conference, University of Tampere (Finland), June 1998; forthcoming in Jo Labanyi (ed.), *Construction Identity in Twentieth-Century Spain Theoretical Debates and Cultural Practice*.

22. See Rosa Montero, 'Political Transition and Cultural Democracy: Coping with the Speed of Change', Graham and Labanyi (eds.), *Spanish Cultural Studies*, pp. 315–20 (p. 317).

23. See Peter Besas, 'The financial structure of Spanish cinema', in *Refiguring Spain: Cinema/Media/Representation*, edited by Marsha Kinder (Durham and London, Duke University Press, 1997), pp. 241–59.